A Man From Corpus Christi

OR

THE ADVENTURES OF TWO BIRD HUNTERS
AND A DOG IN TEXAN BOGS

BY DR. A. C. PEIRCE

ILLUSTRATED WITH TEN PICTOGRAPHS BY NO SPECIAL ARTIST

Copano Bay Press
2008

First Enlarged Edition,
after a Limited Edition of 254 copies

ISBN 978-0-9767799-7-1

CONTENTS

PUBLISHER'S NOTE

The process of editing and designing a book is one that demands the editor become intimately acquainted with the material at hand, at very least from a technical perspective. It is often a game in which fonts, page counts, white space and the author's every word seem to conspire against you at every turn as you try to perfect the layout and create a readable tome. The process requires reading the same material repeatedly until rote memorization appears inevitable. And it is, at times, very easy to lose sight of the essential things that the book aims to do—educate and entertain. This was not so with *A Man From Corpus Christi*. Reviewing each word and paragraph was enjoyable because Peirce's prose is so engaging and the story so amusing. I now count it among my favorite Texas books.

Before taking umbrage to some of the language used in this book, the reader is asked to remember that these events occurred but two decades after the close of the Civil War. Priour and Peirce were men for whom the Civil War, Reconstruction and the scars of both were very real—not just a chapters in an U.S. history textbook. Each man had his own racial vernacular, shaped by geography, life experience and socioeconomic forces. The language used in the text is very much a part of its educational and historical relevance, and an account of life in South Texas in 1887 wouldn't be accurate without it. The potentially offensive words have not been edited for political correctness. To do so, I feel, would be an awkward and unnecessary attempt at rewriting history.

This book would most likely never have come to my attention were it not for another "man from Corpus Christi"—Jim Moloney. Jim, a friend with a penchant for Corpus Christi history, books, postcards and other ephemera, has spoken fondly of this book to me for several years and it was at his suggestion that the book has now been republished. Not only did he grant me access to his copy of the rare first edition of the book, but he was kind enough to provide an introduction, the biographies of Mr. Priour and Mr. Peirce and the map of their travels, all of which add much to the value of this edition.

The image of John M. Priour, as well as the bird's-eye-view map of Corpus Christi used in this edition appear owing to the generous assistance of Mr. Herb Canales and the Corpus Christi Central Library. The former image is part of the library's Doc McGregor image collection, and the latter is housed in the Inez Sterling Adams South Texas Historical Gallery at the Central Library. We are also grateful to Mr. Canales for his help in securing the photo of Dr. A. C. Peirce.

The publisher would further like to thank Mr. Stanley D. Casto of Seguin, Texas for providing vital biographical information on John M. Priour and directing us to further sources of such information.

Appreciation is due to the following individuals for their kind assistance in helping to locate valuable biographical information on Dr. A. C. Peirce: Ms. Debra Tirrell of the East Providence Public Library; Mr. Adam Misturado of the Providence Public Library; and Mr. Kenneth S. Carlson of the State Archives Division of the Office of the Secretary of State of Rhode Island.

Michelle M. Haas, Managing Editor
Seven Palms - Rockport, Texas

AN INTRODUCTION

As a collector of Corpus Christi area books and ephemera, I first discovered *A Man from Corpus Christi* years ago in a bookseller's catalog. I was intrigued by the tale and especially by the description of the countryside near Corpus Christi in the late 1800s. The area, then as now, was teeming with many species of birds, mammals and reptiles. It was a fishing and hunting paradise. The man from Corpus Christi, John Marion Priour, was a hunter and guide to many ornithologists who came to South Texas to collect bird skins and eggs for their personal collections. Many of these collections have since formed the basis for museum and university collections in the Midwest and Northeast.

As the United States prospered in the Gilded Age, after the Civil War and Reconstruction, the second half of the Industrial Revolution generated immense wealth. This wealth allowed men of a certain class to pursue individual interests with a well-funded passion. Some collected art, others became world travelers. The aesthetic appeal of birds combined with the abundance of bird life in unsettled areas compelled some to become ornithologists. In the 1880s, being an ornithologist meant not only studying birds, their habitats and lives in books and in the field, but also collecting their skins, eggs and nests. Many came to Corpus Christi and South Texas because of its wide variety of bird habitats—from shorelines to grasslands, forests, brush country and near-desert. Located at the narrowing of the continent, South Texas hosts the confluence of several migratory bird routes, which afforded visiting ornithologists an opportunity to see the greatest variety of bird species in North America. Thus, many made their way to South Texas in an effort to add new species to their collections. One such visitor was Dr. A. C. Peirce, who authored *A Man from Corpus Christi*.

The landscape in and around Corpus Christi in the late 19th century would be an alien sight to modern residents. The 1890 U.S. Census shows Nueces County to have a population of only 8,093 residents, and these residents were spread over quite a large area. Nueces County then was much larger, containing today's Kleberg and Jim Wells counties. Many familiar Coastal Bend cities did not exist in 1890—Kingsville, Aransas Pass, Ingleside, Robstown and Bishop to name a few. Corpus Christi had been connected to the rest of the United States by railway in 1887 when the San Antonio & Aransas Pass Railway was built across the mouth of Nueces Bay. The train trip to San Antonio by rail took seven hours. Roads, such as they were, were mere horse and wagon trails between the few towns of the region. In some places, they were nothing more than a mere plow furrow leading to a small populated area. The large ranches of the area had not yet been subdivided into farms, and much of the area remained wetlands and natural habitat.

This book offers valuable insight into the wilderness and living conditions in South Texas of a bygone era. It also plainly illustrates the difficulties of being an ornithologist. The author provides an hilarious narration of his adventures with Priour and his dog, Absalom. He also provides insight into the people who inhabited this near-wilderness.

Finding an original copy of the book, *A Man from Corpus Christi*, is no easy undertaking. It is held in less than one hundred libraries worldwide and rarely found for sale on the rare book market. When a copy is located, however, it is expensive and sometimes in poor condition. As such, Peirce's valuable narrative is not readily available to today's readers. Consequently, it was decided, with the help of Michelle Haas and Mark Pusateri of Copano Bay Press to republish it, for it is a window into a very different era of South Texas history. In republishing the book, we wished to include biographical information on the author, A. C. Peirce and his guide, John M. Priour. Tracking down the information used here proved rather challenging. After one hundred years, little information on either was readily available—even on the internet.

I hope that you enjoy "the adventures of two bird hunters and a dog in Texas bogs".

Jim Moloney
Corpus Christi, Texas

ABOUT
THE MAN FROM CORPUS CHRISTI

John Marion Priour (1848–1931)

John M. Priour was once well-known in Corpus Christi, Texas. He was a leading guide for naturalists searching for collectible species of birds and fauna in the area. While never a member of the American Ornithologists Union, he was closely identified with a number of prominent American ornithologists. Today, Priour is forgotten. Though his work is sometimes cited in ornithological papers, the general public has no knowledge of John Marion Priour. Most of Priour's notes on birds, however, are included in Harry C. Oberholser's book, *Bird Life of Texas* published in 1974.

J. M. Priour's father, Gene M. Priour, was born in Rennes, France, in 1812 and came to the United States in 1836, landing at Mobile, Alabama. His mother, Rosalie R. Hart, was born in Wexford County, Ireland, in 1825, and brought to this country by her parents in 1834, with a party of colonists who were to settle at San Patricio near the Nueces River. The party landed at Copano Bay, about 30 miles north of present day Corpus Christi. After her father died of cholera, contracted aboard the ship, Miss Hart was taken by her mother to Mobile, Alabama, where she received her education. There she met and married Gene M. Priour in 1844.

John Marion Priour was born in Mobile, Alabama on March 3, 1848. In 1852, according to his own account, he "was brought to Texas and landed on the beach at Corpus Christi Bay." Here, Priour with his parents and seven siblings, settled in what was then a frontier town. Young Priour turned his hand to a variety of pursuits. Starting at the age of nineteen as a clerk in a grocery and dry goods store in Corpus Christi, he spent a couple of years in his employer's interests in Mexico. Eventually he returned to take charge of his father's ranch on the Aransas River.

For the next few years he seems to have led the frontier life of those days, looking after his father's ranch, driving cattle to market, sometimes to Louisiana. He recounted that he "was with the Volunteer Rangers six years at the time our pistols were the law, judge, and jury". At one time he worked as engineer on the new Tex-Mex railroad that had just been built from Corpus Christi to Laredo, and then learned the trade of carpentry. In October 1877, during one of his trips to Louisiana, he married Margaret Elida Wanning, of Morgan City and brought her back to Corpus Christi near which they made their home.

While, by all accounts, Priour was a born hunter and outdoorsman, he did not seem to have been particularly interested in the birds or mammals teeming around him, at least as a collector, until he was over the age of thirty and then quite by accident. Priour's introduction to ornithological collecting is recounted in Frank M. Chapman's *Autobiography of a Bird Lover*.

> A born hunter, his field had been extended from game birds to "Chippies" through a chance meeting with Colonel N. S. Goss, author of the standard *Birds of Kansas*. One morning in 1878, Goss stopped at Priour's for a drink of water. He had a Caracara and a Marsh Hawk flung over his shoulder, birds which, to a hunter, are as Vultures. As a joke on his caller's supposed ignorance, Priour said, 'You have some fine soup birds there.' Goss took that remark in his kind, gentle way, patiently explained why he was shooting such apparently worthless birds...Priour's evident interest led to his engagement as a guide and to his subsequent employment by Sennett and other ornithologists.

Precisely when Priour learned to stuff birds, and began to collect them and their eggs is not known, but this friendship with Col. Goss, begun quite by accident, seems to have been maintained. Priour writes that "in 1881, Col. N. S. Goss of Neosho Falls came to Corpus and we collected and mounted quite a lot of specimens."

In 1882 Goss's brother, Capt. B. F. Goss of Pewaukee, Wisconsin, came to Corpus Christi, and was joined by noted ornithologist George B. Sennett. Of this trip, Priour writes that "[they] collected from the Rio Grande to the mouth of the Guadalupe River." He continued to collect eggs either with Capt. Goss, or on his behalf, until 1886, and collected skins for Sennett until 1891. The June 5, 1883 issue of the *Corpus Christi Caller* newspaper noted:

> Mr. John Priour, who it will be remembered went the rounds of the press as the champion hunter, is now engaged in collecting different birds and eggs for B. F. Goss of Pewaukee, Wisconsin, and N. S. Goss, Naturalists. He has a territory to work up which extends from the Rio Grande to the Guadalupe rivers. He has made a shipment to those gentlemen of 35 different kinds of eggs, and now has on hand 87, besides a number of birds, which he will shortly ship. The winter months he devotes to hunting and the remainder of the year he devotes to research for birds and eggs.

Col. Goss's collection of mounted birds, originally in the Kansas State Capitol later was transferred to the Museum of the Kansas State Historical Society at

Topeka. Capt. Goss's egg collection is housed at the Milwaukee Public Museum, although he gave a great many eggs to the United States National Museum at Washington. A good many of Sennett's skins are also in Washington, but such skins as he possessed at the time of his death passed to the American Museum of Natural History in New York.

Priour began collecting specimens for George B. Sennett in 1884 and was soon providing specimens to him on a regular basis. In the spring of 1887, Priour was employed to collect specimens between Corpus Christi and the Brazos River to the north. Leaving on April 7, he traveled through Rockport to Refugio and Bee counties to Victoria, where he shipped a box of specimens. He then proceeded to the Navidad River, Colorado River, Caney Creek and Brazoria to the mouth of the Brazos River, arriving on May 21. Returning via Eagle Lake to Brazoria and thence to Corpus Christi, he reached home on June 11.

While the thousands of specimens collected by Priour were invariably labeled with such data as was necessary, he seems never to have thought of putting on his own name as collector.

That Sennett thought a lot of Priour is evident, for Dr. J. A. Allen, in his account of Sennett's life, in the *Auk*, January 1901, wrote:

> In this same year (1887) he sent Mr. J. M. Priour to the region of the lower Brazos River, and later to explore the coast region, or Tamaulipan district, of northeastern Mexico. Priour made a wagon trip from Corpus Christi to Tampico in 1888, amassing large collections, which threw much light on the faunal character of this then little-known region, and helped to establish the boundaries of the Tamaulipan Fauna. As the country about Tampico proved very unhealthful, Mr. Priour nearly lost his life there from malaria and was ill for several months. The next season, 1889, to enable him to recuperate, and to continue his work in a more salubrious region, Mr. Sennett sent him to the eastern base of the Sierra Madre, where for several months he collected in the vicinity of Monterrey. Priour reported that they had collected over 600 birds and that he was anxious to get home after over two months absence. The results of Priour's two important Mexican expeditions unfortunately were never published.

The 1880's seem to have been a productive decade for Priour, ornithologically speaking, for, in the spring of 1884 he collected with Joseph L. Hancock from March 16 to April 1, and in 1887 with George Benners of Philadelphia, and there were a number of others.

Dr. Frank M. Chapman writes:

> I lived with John Priour either at his home or with him in camp from March 16 to April 25, 1891. His striking personality, his knowledge of

the country, and his enthusiasm as a collector made my month with him stand out as one of the most enjoyable of my collecting experience.

In 1894, Forest & Stream Publishing Co. published *A Man from Corpus Christi; or The Adventures of Two Bird Hunters and a Dog in Texas Bogs by* Dr. A. C. Peirce. Of Priour, Peirce wrote that

> ...Mr. Priour was a professional hunter; He made hunting his whole business the year around, and as his jaunts extended in every direction, he was well acquainted with the country for miles about Corpus Christi. He also collected specimens of natural history for various parties, and as my principal object in visiting the country was to secure such specimens myself, I could not have found a man better fitted for my companion.

Vernon Bailey, who was the Chief Field Naturalist and Senior Biologist of the Department of Agriculture's Biological Survey Bureau said of Priour:

> On April 13, 1900, Mrs. Bailey and I first met Priour and his son at Corpus Christi, and he went around with us for several days on trips to the flooded bottoms of the Nueces River to get Wild Turkeys, and down along the coast and Laguna Madre for water and shore birds. He was a taxidermist and skin collector, and had for years been in the business of collecting plumage for the millinery trade with Armstrong, Watson, and others. He had been with many well-known ornithologists and helped them collect, and knew birds fairly well... He was a kindly, helpful friend with the interests and enthusiasm of a real naturalist. His contributions to science in both ornithology and mammalogy were far more important than some of those that get more credit.

From 1900 to 1916, after the trade in plumage had become a thing of the past and collectors were becoming rare, Priour seems to have spent most of his time working as a carpenter, either in Corpus Christi, or in other parts of Texas, building oil well derricks or doing his bit during the war by helping on the buildings for the Army Camp at San Antonio. After Mrs. Priour's death in 1916, he closed his old home and went to live with one of his daughters.

Mr. N. A. Francis of Brookline, Mass., made successive egg collecting trips with Priour in the springs of 1919–1921. He had told ornithologist Frederich H. Kennard so much about Priour that, in February, 1922, Kennard and his son Bob, while collecting along the coast of Texas, stopped off at Corpus Christi for the sole purpose of meeting Priour. They spent five enjoyable days in his company, exploring the country near Calallen. Together they tramped the shores of the Nueces River, and sailed down the Laguna Madre to Bird and Padre Islands.

Kennard was so charmed by Priour's delightful personality, his youthful enthusiasm (he was 75 at the time), and above all, by his kindliness, that they carried on a somewhat desultory correspondence afterwards, even though the old man hated letter-writing. After Kennard had provided Priour with the necessary permits, Priour collected a few birds for him, as well.

The late Walter R. Savory of Wareham, Mass., seems to have been the last one to have gone camping and egg collecting with him. He wrote that in the spring of 1927, when Priour was 79 years old…

…we collected together for some months, Uncle John going with me in my auto and camping wherever we happened to stop. He gave me all the sets he found. I never ceased to admire the natural-born courtesy that distinguished him. It was a privilege to know him.

Of Priour's character, Kennard wrote:

Modest, unassuming, generous to a fault, always ready to do anything for anybody at any time, I think it was his kindliness that most attracted me, and as an example of this, I would like to tell of one personal incident. It has been the custom, these many years, for my friends and neighbors to gather at my home in Massachusetts on New Year's Eve and together, see the Old Year out and the New Year in. As part of the decorations there is always hanging from a beam in the front hall a sprig of mistletoe.

Now mistletoe grows luxuriantly about Corpus Christi, and one day while with Priour, I told him of our custom, and wished that I might have, on these occasions, just such a wonderful clump as we happened to be looking at, to hang in my hall. Nothing further was said about it at the time, and I had forgotten the incident until, a couple of days before New Year's, a large box was received from Texas containing just such a clump of mistletoe. And each year since then, such boxes have arrived. Not only that, but before he died the old man asked his daughter to continue the custom, because I had been his friend.

John Marion Priour died March 14, 1931, at Corpus Christi. He was survived by one son, John W. "Doc" Priour of Hebbronville, Texas, and two daughters, Mrs. Elizabeth Roark of Corpus Christi and Mrs. Nora Lee Cunningham of Calallen, Texas. He was predeceased by his wife and by two children, Thomas and Marguerite Charlotte Priour.

ABOUT THE AUTHOR

Arthur Clarence Peirce
(1858–1903)

Arthur C. Peirce was born of colonial New England stock on November 15, 1858. at Hingham, Mass. Raised and educated in the public schools there, Peirce chose medicine as his profession. He studied at Rush Medical College in Chicago, the College of Physicians and Surgeons in Chicago and Kentucky Medical School in Louisville, from which he received his M.D. in June 1883. After practicing medicine for several years in Dighton, Mass., he settled in Brownville, Rhode Island in 1895 with his wife, Idella.

Though Dr. Peirce was embarking on a successful career in medicine, he also had great interest in ornithology. He thus found the time and resources to take an extended bird-hunting trip to South Texas in November 1886 through mid-1887. Upon returning home, he regaled friends with his adventures hunting with John M. Priour, a respected guide for leading ornithologists of the day. Priour and his dog, Absalom, provided many a memorable moment for Peirce and he eventually wrote of his adventure. The narrative was published in 1894 by Forest and Stream Publishing, at the time the leading publisher of tales of the outdoors.

Dr. Peirce practiced medicine in Riverside, near Providence, Rhode Island, after moving there in 1897. He was known as a skilled physician and was in high demand in the community. Peirce committed suicide on July 26, 1903 at 45 years of age. He is buried at Barrington, Rhode Island. Following is a transcript of his obituary in the *Providence Evening Bulletin* of July 27, 1903:

A SAD ENDING
Suicide of Dr. Arthur C. Peirce at Riverside.
SHOT HIMSELF IN THE LEFT BREAST AT HIS HOME.
Act of Self-Destruction Followed Nervous Breakdown.

HE HAD BEEN UNABLE TO PRACTICE FOR OVER TWO YEARS.
FINANCIAL REVERSES FOLLOWED IN THE TRAIN OF HIS ILLNESS, THE WHOLE COMBINING TO MAKE HIM EXCEEDINGLY DESPONDENT—HIS WIFE, WHO HAD BEEN AWAY DURING THE AFTERNOON, FOUND THE BODY ON THE FLOOR ON HER RETURN.

Dr. Arthur C. Peirce, formerly a leading and successful physician in Riverside and vicinity, committed suicide by shooting himself in the left breast, at his home, corner of Bullock's Point and Oak Avenues, early last evening. Dr. Peirce, who was about 45 years of age, and who had for two years and a half been unable to practice because of breaking down of his health, was alone in the house at the time he committed the act of self-destruction.

The doctor's wife had been in this city a portion of the day to attend to a business matter. She returned home about 6:45 o'clock and then made the shocking discovery that her husband was either dead or dying, as his body lay on the floor of his bedroom in a pool of blood. She ran to the Riverside Pharmacy, two blocks away, and called Druggist A. E. Remington to the house. Mr. Remington, finding the body still warm, hastily summoned Dr. A. E. Platt, who immediately saw that the unfortunate man was beyond human aid.

Medical Examiner George F. Allison of E. Providence was notified and promptly responded. He found that Dr. Peirce had shot himself once with a .38 caliber revolver, the bullet having entered the left breast just above the second rib, and had passed downward close to the heart. There had been profuse hemorrhage from the wound. The body lay face downward, partly across the threshold of a small closet opening out of the bedroom. He was but partly clad, the garments consisting of underclothing, trousers and a nightshirt.

Upon the floor, near the head, were two moistened towels, but to what use, if any, these had been put, was not plain. Dr. Allison detected a strong odor of chloral at the mouth of the suicide. He found no evidence of anything but a case of suicide, and so gave permission for the customary preparation of the body by an undertaker. Mrs. Peirce, who is a young woman, was in such an intensely nervous condition that she was taken care of at the home of friends in the neighborhood.

The sad affair caused a profound sensation in Riverside, where the doctor had made many warm friends during the half dozen years that he had been engaged there in active practice. He was a physician of such skill as is seldom found in a small community, and he was also liked very much as a man. Mrs. Peirce has been closely identified with the social life of the place and the couple formerly kept servants and several horses. Less than three years ago, however, Dr. Peirce's health broke down, after a winter of uncommonly severe work. One night in particular he was called out of the house six times between bed time and sunrise. He went to Maine and stayed there a long while, but when he came back he picked up so slowly that few of his friends believed he would ever be able to practice again. Nervous prostration was given as the cause of his condition.

A few weeks ago he seemed to be much stronger and brighter, and the improvement was noted with pleasure by his friends. But the long illness and the consequent heavy expense and an unfortunate run of bad luck probably had affected him to an extent hardly realized by most others. He disposed of one horse, discharged his coachman and house servant, then one horse died and later the other, valued at several hundred dollars, also died, and to cap it all, it is said, he was informed within a few days of the foreclosure of a mortgage upon his real estate. Literally driven to the wall financially, unstrung by his long illness and perhaps resorting to some powerful antidote to deaden his realization of his desperate condition, he resorted to the bullet. It was a sad ending of a career which had promised much only a few years ago.

Dr. Peirce was a Mason and was a member of two or three Orders, but was rarely seen except when following the duties of his profession. He leaves only a widow, the union never having been blessed with children. He and Mrs. Peirce had a large circle of acquaintances in Barrington, where they formerly resided.

CORPUS CHRISTI, TEXAS IN 1887

When Dr. Peirce came to South Texas, the city looked like this view dated 1887. The view shows the city looking toward the west. Corpus Christi had a population of nearly 4,400. It was served by two railroads—the Tex-Mex connecting to Laredo and Mexico and the San Antonio & Aransas Pass to San Antonio. Dr. Peirce arrived on the latter, which, other than by horse or boat, was the only way to reach the city by land from the rest of the United States. Corpus Christi occupied an area of two blocks by twelve blocks below the bluff and several blocks along and behind the bluff, from today's Cooper's Alley north to Belden Street. Priour lived about one and one-half miles west of the city just to the south of the salt lake pictured in the upper center of the bird's-eye-view.

Some of this adventure took place in Nueces Bay and the Nueces flats. The bay is in the upper right and the flats are behind the Bay on the horizon. Just to the north, (right-hand side) out of the view is North Beach, which was mostly unoccupied in 1887. Beyond that was the reef road across the mouth of Nueces Bay. The road, a natural reef made up of oyster shells, was about 18 inches below the surface of the water and snaked across the bay. The reef was fordable nearly all the time.

This bird's-eye-view map was drawn by Augustus Koch, an itinerant illustrator who travelled the country for thirty years after the Civil War, applying the map-making skills he learned serving the Union during the War. Its inclusion in this volume is courtesy of the Inez Adams South Texas Historical Gallery, Corpus Christi Central Library.

CAMP ON THE NUECES

Dr. Frank M. Chapman is pictured above at the camp on the Nueces River which he shared with John M. Priour in 1891. Dr. Chapman was the Assistant to the Curator of Birds and Mammals at the American Museum in New York City. During his 44-year career at the Museum, Chapman oversaw the growth of its ornithological collections to the worldwide scope it presents today.

This scene is similar to how Peirce and Priour's camp, as described in this text, may well have appeared. In this photograph, we see Chapman posed in front of a more professionally-made tent than the homemade one described in this book and shared by Priour and Peirce several years earlier. Hanging from the tent is the Wild Turkey that Chapman obtained on the trip. Note the rifles propped against the wagon and the chest at the entrance to the tent, used for storage and writing while in the field.

Chapman wrote in his *Autobiography of a Bird Lover*, "Every waking hour of my week's trip with Priour was filled with interesting and novel experiences...He was a happy-go-lucky, joyous companion and a keen hunter. The country was unsettled, wild it seemed to me, and after the first day wild cat, coyote and Wild Turkey tracks were frequent. On one long stretch of straight road we saw six Turkeys cross ahead of us. Priour stopped, unhitched one of the horses and, using it for a blind, stalked the birds and shot a fine year-old male...From March 15th to April 25th I observed 197 species. A large proportion was new to me, and my ornithological experience was thus greatly widened."

MAP SHOWING PEIRCE AND PRIOUR'S TRAVELS THROUGH SOUTH TEXAS IN 1887

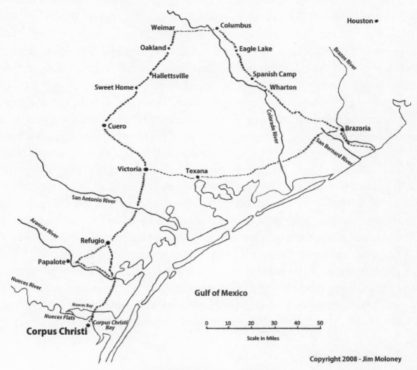

Map, Courtesy of Jim Moloney

John Priour left Corpus Christi at 6 p.m. on Thursday, April 6, 1887 on a nine-week hunting trip for birds to send to ornithologist George B. Sennett. He was accompanied by Dr. A. C. Peirce, who was building his own collection of ornithological specimens. After crossing Nueces Bay on the curving underwater reef road, they met with their first misadventure when their horses stampeded, spilling the entire contents of their heavily loaded wagon in the darkness of the night.

Following crude roads, trails, and faint plow furrows they made their way to Texana on Lavaca Bay. Priour and Peirce found the old city intact, but without residents. When the railroad bypassed Texana for Edna, the old port city had been deserted. From Texana they made their way to the Brazos River, which they followed to its mouth at the Gulf of Mexico on May 21. After foiling man-eating Texas mosquitoes with a ring of fire, they journeyed to Columbus through the swamps of southeast Texas. They finally made it back to Corpus Christi on June 11. The total trip covered approximately four hundred miles.

ABSALOM

Friends who have had the courage to read this book in the manuscript, and to read it through, have quarreled with me over its name. The true hero of the story they aver is the dog Absalom, and he should have given title to it. The interest, they claim, centers in him, in his canine eccentricities, his wonderful memory, his patient endurance, and above all his faithful defense or chaperoning, as it were, of those thrown under his protection. All of these they declare make him the central figure of the play in which the human actors—the Man from Corpus Christi and the Author—were but subordinate characters, acting their parts only to develop his. The book then, my friends contend, should have been given some such title as "Honest Absalom" or "Absalom the Great."

They may be right as to the chief interest of the story, but to me their advice seems a waste of sentimental and poetic effusion. They certainly manifest a sympathy for the dog which I confess I do not share. Time, which heals all wounds, has not yet softened my heart for him. Much as I love the Man from Corpus Christi, I cannot bring myself to love his dog. If Absalom here appears as the hero, this is not in consequence of any deliberate intention on my part, but is to be accounted for by the fact that I have taken pains to tell everything as it actually happened. For the tale that is told is loaded with great truths, and I am convinced that Absalom's heroic qualities cannot glow more brightly from the pages that follow than does the brightness of the truth itself.

CHAPTER I
IN WHICH WE GET ACQUAINTED

Late one November evening I stepped from the cars at Corpus Christi, and taking a cab, was driven through mud, mire and rain a mile and a half to the house of John M. Priour. Mr. Priour and his family had retired for the night, and, being wholly unacquainted with the man, I wondered how he would feel about being called out of bed by a stranger. He had neither seen nor heard of me, and it seemed not just the right thing for me to attempt an introduction at such an hour. But shortly after a rap at his door my misgivings vanished, for with true Southern hospitality the man welcomed me to his home and offered me lodging under his roof. Outside, the night was a cheerless one, but my host stirred up the drowsy fire in the large open fire-place, and seating ourselves by it, we discussed matters connected with my visit, and various social topics. The man I had thus introduced myself to was pleasant and agreeable, and seated comfortably by his log fire, the rain beating fiercely against the roof and sides of the house, we thought little of time until near midnight. At that hour I retired to the bed which had been provided for me and slept sweetly until morning.

Mr. Priour was a professional hunter; he made hunting his whole business the year around, and, as his jaunts extended in every direction, he was well acquainted with the country for miles about Corpus Christi. At this season of the year his game was principally wildfowl, and he was constantly making visits to various lakes and other resorts of these birds, being gone from home five and ten days at a time. He also collected specimens in natural history for various parties, and as my principal object in visiting the country was to secure such specimens myself, I could not have found a man better fitted for my companion, and I made arrangements to travel and hunt with him during my stay.

From a neighbor I rented an unoccupied shed, which was to be my headquarters, the landlord kindly furnishing corn husks enough to make a nice soft bed in one corner. I needed no pillows, for the house had been built upon posts which time had now disintegrated to such an extent that they had partly collapsed, allowing the building to drop upon the ground at one side, while the opposite side was two feet in air. With my head to the upper side, I must sleep nicely. The door of this shed was on the grounded side and at first refused to open more than a small space; but by digging away the ground it was made to swing open its whole width. The roof of my new home was quite leaky, but the owner informed me that during some rainstorm I could chalk the floor where the water dripped, and by doing so I could learn just where it would be unsafe to place perishable articles.

Nueces Flats

About a week after my arrival at Corpus Christi, Mr. Priour harnessed his two horses, Whitie and Gruya, and with a plentiful supply of ammunition, we started for the Nueces Flats. Our road was mostly through a country covered with a low growth of mesquite and weesatche brush, where pasture fences were much more numerous than houses, of which we saw few. The scraggy growth of brush on each side of the road was more or less inhabited by birds, and we secured several fine specimens. Twelve or fifteen miles from our starting place, we left the beaten road, and traveling four or five miles over a rough and hilly stretch of land, crossed the Nueces River and camped a few miles beyond.

Above the junction of the river with the bay is a large area of low marshy surface; this is the Nueces Flats, which include several thousand acres of land and water. In hundreds of places on the north side of the river, the earth is depressed below the level of the stream; and these depressions, filled with water, are, in places, only separated from each other and the large stream by slight elevations. Replacing the land by water, and the water by land, Nueces Flats would be a large lake containing countless islands, more or less connected by narrow isthmuses. As a rule, the bottoms of these small bodies of water are firm, but a few of those nearest the river are decidedly boggy. On each side of the river, and between the water and the grass-covered land, is a space perhaps twenty yards in width, which is made up of bottomless mud. To venture on to this mud is simply to venture into it, and as it is seemingly without limit in depth, one might better try to walk on the ocean, so far as danger is concerned. To appreciate what "bogged" means, one must have the experience of being in the mud waist deep, feet firmly pressed together, gradually sinking, and no way of deliverance but by turning on the face or side and paddling out regardless of toilet arrangements; depending upon the increase of surface in these positions, to keep mouth and nose out of the semi-fluid slump.

Mr. Priour had spent many days tramping over these flats, and was well acquainted with every foot of the surface. We found wild geese and ducks in abundance; nearly every one of the small ponds was well stocked with them; and my companion knew the exact way to approach each flock unseen. Gulls and terns were also plentiful, and late in the afternoon of the day of our arrival, we killed many fine specimens. These birds frequent the place in search of food, which they find about the strip of mud next the river; and as they were all killed while flying, they almost invariably fell into the water or mire.

After having dropped a good number, we proceeded to fish them out. I secured the few that my gun had shot, by dragging driftwood into the bog and building piers out to them; this method was slow, but it accomplished results in time. Mr. Priour, however, had had more experience in the business, and deliberately removing his coat and hat, he crawled and wallowed around in the mud on his hands and knees in a way that astonished me. Fully one-half of his body was below the surface, and at times it appeared as if he would drop out of sight. With his teeth he seized each bird by the wing, and when his jaws could open no further, he paddled ashore and let go his load. In this way he made several trips, finally bringing out the last bird; and when he had finished his labor, nothing but a pair of eyes was in sight to show that the reeking mass of black mud contained a human being. Little did I think that before leaving Texas, I should many times be as muddy as he was on this occasion.

In a Labyrinth

By the time we had collected our birds, the sun had set, and shouldering the game, we started for our camp two miles away. Here I made a great mistake by taking a route different from that of my companion. He knew the way well, but as our wagon stood on a hill and in plain sight, I thought there could be no trouble in navigating to it. After walking but a short distance, I brought up before one of the innumerable ponds, and naturally started to go around it, only to find a second one in my path, with its edge leading back toward the river again. Retracing my steps, I passed around the other end of the first I had met; but had not gone very far when I was confronted by yet another pond, which, as I tried to circumnavigate it, I found was connected by a strait with a still larger body of water.

This was discouraging. It was now quite dark, and after traveling far enough to have gone to camp twice, I was still only about half-way there; and it seemed that whatever course I might take, sooner or later it would bring me to the long side of a pond. I could see the campfire that my partner had made, and I wished with all my heart that I had kept with him. Finally I became desperate. That camp-fire was as much mine as Mr. Priour's, and I wanted its company; and plunging into the water before me, I waded through.

I was wet now, and fixing my eyes on the bright light, I steered straight for camp, wading ponds and mudholes as often as they crossed my path. I wore a brand new pair of rubber boots, and had been congratulating myself on how dry they would keep my feet; but as many of the ponds were waist deep, my boots soon filled; and at every step on the land the mixture of mud and water squirted up to my neck. When I reached camp, Mr. Priour laughed at my experience. He had made the large fire to guide me, and at the time of my arrival was lying by the blaze, watching a duck which was cooking in our kettle. He had removed his clothing and shaken out some of the mud, but was still as wet as a sponge. I emptied my boots and wrung out my pantaloons, and put them on again. We ate a hearty supper of fried duck, and after a long smoke rolled into our blankets for the night. Covered with mud and wet to my waist, I felt like an oyster dipped in batter and ready to fry, only instead of frying I was shivering.

We spent two days and three nights on the flats, securing a good number of bird skins and ducks; and on the morning of the third day drove up to the river nearly to the ferry by which we had crossed a few days before. There were plenty of drift logs by this stream, and Mr. Priour wished to get a load of them for firewood. Emptying the wagon of all its contents, we piled in the wood. Mr. Priour said, that as the distance was great, we had better take all the wagon could carry; and he shocked me in piling it on so high, log after log being put on as though it was to be a load of hay. These logs were anything but straight, and when enough had been packed on, it was hardly possible to see either wagon-box or wheels, for the branches projected at all quarters. On top of all this heap we put our camp furniture, and I was invited to ride over the ferry and hold the things from spilling; but this I declined to do.

Crossing the Ferry

At the place of crossing the river, the water is about ten feet below the top of the bank, and the pitch of this slope is frightfully steep; I therefore preferred to walk carefully behind, and remain upon the bank until the wagon was on board the boat. Taking the lines and walking beside the horses, Mr. Priour drove to, and over the bank. There being no breaching to the harness, the instant the wheels started down the declivity, the horses made a dash to get out of the way of the wagon; and the whole outfit struck the boat like an avalanche on wheels. Thankful was I that I had remained on the bank, for the air was filled with ducks, geese, coffee-pots and logs. Several articles of culinary use, including, our kettle, went overboard and out of sight; but with a pole we fished out the most of our birds. There was one log in the bottom of the wagon which was much crooked, sticking out behind like a crank. This crank we had turned to one side when loading, but in the slide down the embankment it had rotated one-fourth of a circle, its end resting on the boat; and, as it was firmly wedged in by the logs above, the after wheels of the wagon were lifted about six inches clear of everything. Of course our load had to be repacked before going further; and we had trouble with it all the way home. It was sundown when we reached Corpus again, and I enjoyed my night's sleep much better in my shed than I had on the flats.

Traveling and hunting thus with my new friend, I passed the winter and a part of spring. Most of our journeys had been short in distance and time; but I became familiar with the scenes about Corpus, and the reserve that is natural between two strangers like Mr. Priour and myself had been overcome. Being alone with each other for days and weeks at a time, we had, in a few months, become as well acquainted as though living in the same neighborhood for years. We had eaten from the same stew-pot, slept under the same blanket, and bogged in the same mire, until almost a part of each other; and I often wondered how my bird-collecting scheme would have terminated, had I not found such an agreeable companion.

CHAPTER II
"I'M FROM CORPUS CHRISTI"

For nearly five months Mr. Priour and myself had been freely exposed to the elements; having had with us on our hunting excursions no protection whatever, with the exception of that offered by our bedding. To be sure, we had never been more than fifty miles from Corpus Christi, and in case of very severe weather, could easily have driven to our headquarters in two days. But now we were contemplating an extended tour up the coast, and feeling the need of something adequate to the occasion, we determined to fabricate a shelter that would serve as a tent. We had had no experience in the tent business, and thought the opportunity to display our inventive qualities a grand one. We had seen tents; knew them to be of various styles—grand, square, upright— but that was the extent of our knowledge.

A day or more was spent in gathering material for our work. We had no canvas, and we wanted none, for our tent was not to be of the canvas variety; in fact, it was to be a variety of everything but canvas.

Our first acquisition was an old blanket, which was followed by cast-off shirts, pantaloons and hats. In fact, everything of a flexible nature that could be secured, we immediately took possession of; and after the accumulation of a pile that in size and quality might have excited envy in a junk dealer, we were ready actually to begin tent making.

Put together, our material was regular patchwork, and crazy at that; but after two days had been patiently spent in quilting, we were proud to be in possession of a pyramidal bag, which we thought might afford some protection in stormy weather. (No one can ever know how many times some of the articles were sewed together and ripped apart again, before finding their final place of duty.)

Mr. Priour had provided himself with a new wagon, and we obtained a full complement of empty boxes, selected with great exactness what to stow in them. We had an iron stew-pot, a coffee-pot, a tin plate and one fork. Not being of fastidious dispositions, we thought these would be enough in that line, for a company of two. Our stock of ammunition was complete, and consisted of one thousand loaded shells besides twenty-five pounds of powder and a hundred pounds of shot. For provisions, we had thirty pounds of hard-bread, and two pounds of coffee. This was rather a small amount of food to start on a long trip with, but we expected to live principally on game that might fall in our way.

At six o'clock P. M. Thursday, April 7, all was in readiness for the journey. I suggested to Mr. Priour that, owing to the lateness of the hour, we postpone our start until the following morning, when we could rise with the sun and leave in daylight. But he was exceedingly unwilling to begin a journey on Friday, and insisted upon our starting this night, even if making only a mile or two before coming to camp.

Our Initial Catastrophe

At seven o'clock P. M., Mr. Priour, his dog Absalom, and myself set out to cross Nueces Bay along the staked trail on the reef, and it was quite dark when we reached the further side. Here the wagon road winds along the edge of the water for a few rods, and meets the railroad at right angles. A team may go further by driving up the steep ascent over the railroad and down the precipitous bank on the other side, or by driving under the timbers of the bridge, between the bay and the bank. The north way, over the hill, does fairly well with a strong team and empty wagon, but a boat cannot be drawn over it. The hill was made to enable teams to cross the railroad, but on both sides it is about as steep as gravel can be piled. On the other hand, the distance between the ground and the timbers of the bridge south of the hill, is too little to allow the passage of a bulky wagon.

Stopping near this crossing, we found that our wagon was too well-filled, and that we should have to remove some of our load before going further; and we were about to do this when without warning, our horses made a dash through the dark passage, and under the bridge. Being frightened by the noise of smashing and falling boxes, the animals started off on a run and strewed the beach with boards, splinters, hard-bread, stew-pots and shot bags. The sound of horses' hoofs gradually became fainter as they increased the distance from us, until noise of a final crash rang out on the night air, piercing our very hearts with grief. Then everything became quiet, and we knew that something had happened. The fearful silence was soon broken by the thundering voice of my companion:

"Did you hear that crash?"

"I heard it."

"Do you know what it was?"

"No. Do you?"

"Yes, I know what it was; it was my gun. The barrels are wrenched from the stock, and the locks are ruined; and what's more, Absalom's killed!"

"How do you know Absalom's killed?"

"How do I know it! Didn't you see him dash off after the team? Didn't you see him grab the horses by the bridle? I tell you, that dog's got them horses or he's killed himself a trying it." Mr. Priour was thoroughly angry, and rich deep words fell from his tongue as he started after the runaways.

Thinking that one could find the team as well as two, I employed myself in gathering up the wrecked cargo and piling it in heaps convenient for collection. This was no light undertaking. The night was dark; the ground was thickly studded with clumps of coarse grass, and by repute the spot was a favorite one for rattlesnakes. Working diligently in the darkness, I trod out camp paraphernalia until I believed all had been recovered. Fortunately I found my pipe, and after unraveling it from a piece of bacon in which it had been woven during its spill, I seated myself upon our box of axle grease, and enjoyed a good smoke, being thankful that I had at least one necessary article left whole. While I was enjoying myself, Absalom emerged from some shrubbery near the bridge, where he had been hiding since the calamity; and, after finding everything quiet, started quickly on after his master.

Absalom is a Snooker

Accompanied by his dog, Mr. Priour soon returned, and his first words were: "Now I'll be dog-on'd if that Absalom ain't a snooker; what do you suppose he was doing when I got down here?"

"I don't know."

"Well, he was holding them horses by the bits, just like a rope tied to a tree. He grabbed hold the minute they struck out, and you can thank him that you ain't got to go to the Brazos River afoot. He's worth his weight in hair oil anytime."

"Where's the wagon?" I asked.

"The wagon's bottom side up in the edge of the bay; and you'd better come down and help get it out, if you don't want to stay here all night."

Righting the wagon was not a very difficult matter, and we soon had our team again attached to it; although the harness had first to be mended in several places. This we were able to do by the light of our lantern which had escaped uninjured. Driving back to the scene of the accident, we proceeded to load up again. This time, however, things were put into the wagon rather promiscuously, as compared with their proper riding places which had earlier been studied out with mathematical precision. Both our guns were safe—lock, stock and barrel— Priour's prophecy to the contrary notwithstanding; and as our ammunition had been spilled from the wagon before reaching the water, we concluded that our belongings had not been so much injured as we first feared.

Driving over rather low land for a mile or more, we came to that part of the bay which is backed by a steep bluff; and taking the road between the foot of the vertical bank and the water, we traveled about a mile further, and entering the "Gulley," camped for the night.

The "Gulley" is a deep cut or ravine in the bluff on the north side of Corpus Christi Bay. At the time of construction of the S. A. & A. P. R. R., the company had sunk a well to obtain water for their men and horses. Near the public road and being the only fresh water source within a radius of several miles, it was a favorite camping place, and was occupied nearly every night by some party of travelers. The spot was familiar to us, for we had camped there many times before.

We had some trouble in making a comfortable bed with our wet blankets; but as it was quite late, and we were somewhat tired, and considerably wet already, we were not overly particular about our bedding being perfectly dry, nor did we care to raise the new tent, just for one night.

After spreading blankets and lying down, I ventured to ask what the probable result would have been, had our start been postponed until Friday morning. On this subject he was reticent, but I reasoned with him that if starting on Thursday brought such accidents as we had that night experienced, a journey commenced on such an unlucky day as Friday, would have brought us to certain extinction before reaching the Gulley. Mr. Priour thereupon consoled himself by relating the case of a friend who began a trip up the country on Friday, and before he had been two days out, lost his dog by the bite of a rattlesnake. This incident which he related put an idea into my head, and I thought that if the dog so lost was of the Absalom variety, it could not have been a very unlucky day for the owner after all; and I felt that if our dog could only have perished on this night, my happiness would have been greatly increased. However, I said nothing to Priour of my thoughts.

Burrowing Owls

Friday morning we took account of stock, repacked our wagon, and after a hasty lunch of hard-bread and coffee, moved out of the Gulley. Our road lay between the bay and the steep bluff. The shore is frequented by thousands of water birds, gulls, terns, waders, etc., and many burrowing owls find natural homes in seams of the perpendicular bluff which rises from forty to fifty feet above the sea level. Mr. Priour told me that a burrowing owl would run into its hole, after it had been killed, and that it was a difficult matter to get one of them. These small birds venture only a short distance from their homes during the daytime, and their color being almost identical with that of the soil of the bank, it is not an easy matter to see them, even when only a few yards away. Sitting by the doorway of their homes, often in pairs, they seem a picture of contentment, and a shame it is to molest them; and as my partner had informed me of their ability to run into their caves after being blown to atoms, we contented ourselves with specimens of less modest and innocent game.

Four or five miles from the Gulley, we ascended the bluff, and obtained a fine view of the bay and the surrounding country, Corpus Christi included. On this elevated land we visited a windmill tank to get fresh water for dinner. The mill was a quarter of a mile from the cliff, and further yet from the bay; but the water was salt, and we decided to drive to another mill a mile further inland.

At this mill we camped for lunch, in a pleasant grove. Hundreds of cattle flocked about us, as thirsty as ourselves from drinking the salty mixture of the other tank.

The pump was out of repair and the reservoir empty. By removing the boards from around the piston rod, we could lower our coffee pot by the harness lines, and draw about a gill of liquid at a time. This water was turbid and unwholesome, but boiling plenty of coffee in it partially concealed its sickening taste.

Coffee, as it is made in Texas, has little resemblance to a typical potion of the same elsewhere. I have drunk coffee concocted by many different camp cooks, and it has always been the same bitter dose, and to me only useful when odorless water was unobtainable. The Texan hunter buys his coffee raw and roasts it over his camp-fire until it is perfectly black and every particle of agreeable aroma and flavor has been dissipated, then he puts it in a shot sack and pounds it on the wagon wheel with the heel of his boot until it is sufficiently reduced. Of this charcoal-like powder he puts perhaps a half-pint into a quart of water and boils from fifteen to thirty minutes, supplying the loss by evaporation with more liquid. This he drinks without milk or sugar. Such a decoction has a taste that one might expect from a broth made of burnt hair and feathers. But the Texan likes it; he calls it coffee, drinks it for coffee, and satisfies himself that he has really drunk a cup of that delicious beverage.

"I'm from Corpus Christi"

After our lunch of hard-bread and coffee we returned to the edge of the bluff and followed its many curves and windings. As I understood the matter, we were on a public road, but the trail we followed disgraced the word.

The chasms and fissures, as well as the main bank, were constantly drawing further back from the water, and thus each team must be driven a little further inland than the one which last preceded it a few days before. As the land was thickly overgrown with brush and small trees, this changing of the road always meant the beating down of many brambles, the upsetting of wagons and breaking of harnesses; for no true and loyal Texan would think of cutting down or removing any obstruction which could in any possible way be driven over. In some other parts of the world a man will turn out for a six-inch tree, go around a vertical-sided mound, or travel a half-mile out of his way to go over a bridge across a slough; but in Texas things are different, and those obstacles would be run into and bent over, climbed up and slid off of, and dived into and wallowed through. A stranger attempting to drive over this road during the night would certainly be pitched into the bay before going a mile.

I well knew that Mr. Priour would have no fear of the bluff, still I could not well refrain from uttering a word of caution, and his reply to such a word was, "Now, I tell you I can drive just as dog-on near that bank as any of 'em; I'm from Corpus Christi!" And several times he did drive so "just dog-on near" that one of the rear wheels dropped over the cliff and ground into the earth for two or three revolutions before the team could be headed into the brush to drag it on top again.

The distance to the water was greater than I cared to fall and have a wagon and pair of horses light in the same place at the same time, but my partner related several instances of parties who had been dumped into the bay forty feet below, and had lived to tell the tale.

We camped in the edge of a growth of live-oaks. After spending a half-hour in cutting tent pegs and poles with our blunt axe, we leveled off the ground and raised the crazy structure for the first time. It was somewhat asymmetrical, but everything in the State was peculiar in this respect, and in its whole make-up the tent was Texan. It had a Texan hat in the center of the back end which bore great resemblance to an artillery target. On one side was the outline of a pair of Texan trousers, and a cursory observer of this feature might have supposed that there was a hole in the tent, and that a man had crawled half-way in, and stuck there with his legs hanging down on the outside. But it was our own handiwork and we were proud of it. After our supper had been eaten, we sat an hour or more by the camp-fire, smoking many a pipe of tobacco in its honor, and constantly admiring its profile so distinctly outlined on the dark shrubbery beyond. Finally we retired, leaving Absalom outside the brush to care for the wagon.

We Evacuate

Upon previous occasions I had felt that in sleeping upon the ground with no covering save our blankets and the stars and clouds, we were more or less exposed to attacks of noxious and venomous animals. I had often fallen asleep, wondering what foe might be in hiding, watching for the closing of my eyes before making an assault. But now we were to sleep under a tent, and it was with a feeling of perfect security and complacency that I lay down, enjoyed another smoke, and then throwing away all care and thoughts of invasion, dropped to sleep. I had been unconscious an hour or more, when, partially coming to my senses, I felt something crawling on me. Opening my eyes, I was startled to find upon my chest, and in close proximity to my face, a full-grown skunk. Suddenly rising up, I precipitated the animal between myself and the door, and ejaculating a common Texan expression, succeeded by the words "Get out of this tent!" I climbed over my sleeping companion, and followed by him, found my way under the back end of the tent, into the open air.

This maneuver, in which Mr. Priour played so active a part, did not awaken the man, and he slept on as peacefully as ever, his hasty exit not disturbing his sleep any more than had my sudden alarm. With some difficulty I aroused him, and opening his eyes and staring about for a few seconds, he inquired: "How'd I come outside? What'd you drag that tent off me for anyway?"

"I didn't drag it off; there's a skunk inside!"

"There's a skunk inside? Well, what's that got to do with my being outside? I'll be dog-on'd if I was ever dragged out of my bed by a skunk before."

Mr. Priour was now wide awake, and raising the back fold of our huge bag, we looked in and beheld Mr. Skunk standing upon my pillow of boots rolled in a coat, as quietly and as much at ease as a cat would be, lying by the fireside in its own home. Our guns were in the wagon, our boots in the tent with His Skunk-ship, and the briers were too thick for us to travel barefooted.

If Mr. Priour had his shoes, he would go to the wagon for his gun. So would I do the same. Mr. Priour would stay and watch the skunk from the back end of the tent, while I slipped around to the front and reached in for his foot-gear. So would I do the same for him. In this manner we debated the subject several minutes, with no result. Meantime the animal within the tent went anywhere and into anything he pleased. Mr. Priour called to his dog: "Absalom! Absalom!" But alas, we had fastened Absalom to the wagon wheel; and he wouldn't have known enough to come to us, had he been free. Finally, on hands and knees we crawled to the wagon and secured our weapons; but when we reached the tent again, the enemy had gone. We now crept into the tent with great caution, fearing the pest might have stowed himself away behind some of our many boxes; but after a diligent search, always moving things at arm's length, we felt, that for a time at least, we were safe again.

Mr. Priour explained that this conduct of the skunk was not unusual in Texas. He said the animals seemed to like to associate with people, and they had been known to get into dwelling houses at night, and to be found sleeping on a bed or rug in the morning. He had also known them to make their bed in the warm ashes of a fire-place, and he did not hesitate to prophesy that our guest would reappear after all was quiet.

This was anything but a pleasant thought. Our bedding was already perfumed to saturation, and I had serious thoughts of climbing some tree, and passing the remainder of the night in the branches, leaving my comrade to arrange matters with the skunk as best he could. But Priour said he would prepare for the reception, should the beast call again.

The Valiant Absalom

Dragging Absalom into the clearing, he made him lie on an empty bag by our front door, as a sentinel, trusting to his keen senses to warn us of the approach of an enemy. Poor, innocent, unsophisticated dog, he had never been outside of his master's door-yard before, and didn't know a skunk from an oyster. His master, though, said he had a wonderful memory, and he knew he could be trusted. I knew there was no doubt about his readiness to attack a skunk, should he see one. He would attack a bear or lion as quickly as he would a flea, evincing more ignorance than courage. But I doubted his liability to awake from less cause than a kick in the ribs.

Mr. Priour lay down upon his reeking blanket, and with genuine imperturbability fell asleep within two minutes; but I could not so easily overcome my fears. Thoughts of the living fire-engine haunted me, and, together with the sickening odor now filling the tent so as to make its sides bag outward instead of in, kept me awake for an hour or more.

But sleep came at last, and with it another scene. I was soon awakened by a scratching sound on the outside of the tent immediately back of my partner's head, and awaking him I called his attention to it. Listening a moment, he exclaimed: "Skunk!" and shouted to the dog: "Sic him! Sic him, Absalom!" A second later we heard Absalom howling with pain. Seizing our guns and rushing outside, we saw the dog rapidly describing a circle in the sand, while the centrifugal skunk was describing a similar circle, of greater dimensions, in the air. After three or four revolutions of the merry-go-around, the skunk's grip tore out of Absalom's ear, and a charge of shot from my partner's gun put an end to the scented creature which had so fiercely obeyed an order given to another. "Sic him! Sic him, Absalom."

After poking the dead animal over and viewing it from all sides, Mr. Priour said, "This ain't the skunk that drove you into hysterics the first time."

"How do you know it isn't?" I asked.

"I know by his visage, and you can count on number one's coming back again before morning."

But the words failed to have the desired effect on me, for I detected the humor in his remarks at once. Creeping under our bag, for the third time this night, we slept peacefully until daylight.

CHAPTER III
IN WHICH WE BUY SOAP

After breakfast, our first duty was to wash the bedding, which was damp and odorous from the preceding night. Taking the blankets to a windmill tank, we put them to soak, and spread them on the ground to dry.

During the forenoon we took long tramps up and down the edge of the thicket, sometimes picking our way into its tangles. But birds were scarce, and we obtained few specimens at this place.

A short distance within the brush, Mr. Priour discovered the abode of a bald eagle, and girding up his loins anew, he wrestled with the immense tree until he reached the nest, forty feet from the ground. He had expected to get a set of eggs, but found instead a young bird. "Ha! ha! I'm in luck this time," he shouted, "young birds beat eggs all holler!" and taking this from the nest, he threw it to the ground, expecting the fall to deprive it of life. Catching on several limbs and easing its fall somewhat, it reached the earth, and smoothing out its ruffled feathers, settled quietly among the brush and leaves, apparently none the worse for its unceremonious descent.

Mr. Priour was soon down from the tree, and going up to the prize, was about to lay hands upon it, when it dashed through the snarled growth and out on to clear land. Declaring that he would not be foiled by a young bird with a dozen broken bones, the man dashed after it. The bird would fly a short distance and wait until its pursuer had almost reached it, when it would be up and away again, each time gaining a little on the angry man. Finally the eagle won the race, and my partner had to content himself with a pair of young Cara Cara eagles, which he had taken from another tree.

This night, before going to sleep, we lowered our tent about six inches, and turning under the edges, weighted them down with guns, stew-pots and other utensils. We endeavored to coax Absalom to sleep near us on the outside but no amount of persuasion would induce him to occupy the clearing again. He'd had enough trouble in there the first night to satisfy him, and crawled away to the wagon.

"Now ain't he a cute one?" said my partner. "He knows the next skunk'll steer clear of our guns, and he's going to defend that wagon."

Lightning not striking twice in the same place, we slept sweetly all night. The next morning we pulled out, and traveling over an almost barren prairie, came to the bay in which empties the Aransas River. Following the river, we came about 4 o'clock to a large reservoir fed by a small stream of clear and tasteless water. On each side of the fresh-water stream were many small groves or *motas*, and in one of them we pitched our tent. In the groves on the opposite side we found spots where one might well wish to live and die.

Absalom's Wonderful Memory

Large trees with interwoven branches almost excluding the direct rays of sun-light, covered the unencumbered ground, making natural halls with the level floor only occupied by the upright trunks; and I wished we were to remain here a week or more. We found small birds quite plentiful, also a few large owls. I admired their taste in selecting such a pleasant locality for homes, and almost envied them their beautiful surroundings.

In the tops of the tall trees under which we had camped, were many nests of the great blue heron. These birds are said to be as graceful in flying as a windmill broken loose from its fastenings, which comparison I believe to be an accurate one. But in alighting they much resemble the action of a boy tumbling off a pair of stilts. The first time I saw one of these birds visit its nest, I could almost have sworn that it had died in the air and fallen into the tree, for they are as likely to bring up on their back or head as upon their feet, and I often thought it strange that their haunts could not be known by broken legs and wings scattered about.

Late in the evening I slipped quietly out from under the trees, hoping to get a shot at one of these birds; but they saw my movements and flew away. Absalom had not seen me when I left the campfire (he being too busy in catching fleas to know anything else), and when I came walking leisurely back, I was surprised to have him seize me by the leg and tear my trousers from the knee down. This made me angry at him, but his master praised him for the act, and marveled at his wonderful memory—probably his memory of the fact that he was to protect the camp from all intruders.

In the afternoon of the following day, we started for the Chiltipin Creek. Crossing the Chiltipin, we took a look at a vacant cabin in which we had spent a cold and stormy night in January. The weather was warm now, but sight of the half-burnt sticks which remained in the low, tumbled down, fire-place just as we had left them, was suggestive of the misery in which we had smoked ourselves nearly blind on that wild night. Driving about a mile further, we camped in a small grove of post-oaks.

Why post-oak timber should be called by that name is an unanswerable ques-tion, for like all other trees that I saw in the country, it grows about as crooked as can be imagined. A much more appropriate name would be hoop-skirt oak.

During the night a severe wind came up from the east, laying our tent down upon us, and tearing the back end into shoe-strings. As might have been ex-pected, the wreck did not awaken my partner, although it left his head freely exposed to the driving wind; and it was only after a thorough shaking that he opened his eyes and assisted me in raising the shelter again.

In the afternoon of the following day, we crossed the Aransas River. While driving along the bed of the stream, we saw a large hole in the bank above us, about twenty feet from the water, and four or five from the top of the ground above. This hole we supposed to contain an owl's nest, and after ascending the bluff, we went back to investigate. Clinging to the stunted grass on the edge of the bank, I let myself down to a narrow shelf of sand, about four feet from the top, and on a level with the hole. Digging a place in the sand for one of my hands, and flattening myself as much as possible, I stooped, and was about to insert my free hand into the opening, when, with a sound like the rushing of a mighty wind, a large owl made its exit. This so startled me, that losing my balance, I slipped off the shelf of sand, and holding a handful of torn up grass roots, plunged down the embankment. Where I struck, the earth was soft and loose, and I was uninjured. Then Mr. Priour let himself down by the lines fastened to the wagon-wheel, searched the cavity and found a pair of young birds.

We camped in a pleasant grove on the river's bank. Nearby were several wild mulberry trees loaded with ripe fruit, and we ate our fill a dozen times while here. These trees were also patronized by hundreds of warblers, and we took several varieties of them to our camp.

Papalote

April 14, we drove into Bee County and camped on the river. Packing up what bird skins we had, and leaving the camp in care of Absalom, we drove to the railroad town of Papalote, to ship our trophies, and do some trading.

The settlement of Papalote consists of one dwelling house, one store and post office combined, and the railroad station; all being closely huddled in a small clearing, and surrounded on all sides by a thick wood. The only outlets of the place appeared to be the railroad track and the path by which we had come, a passage cut through the timber, and not much the better from wear.

The store and post office commanded the greater part of our attention. We purchased some coffee and grain, and after a long consultation between Priour and myself in regard to advisability, etc., we decided to invest in a cake of soap. Making our want known to the grocery man, he proceeded to attack a large lump of yellow something with a chisel and hammer. This lump was about as large as a bushel, and I could not remember having seen soap on sale in such style before. After chiseling a while, the man held in his hand a piece of the substance, weighing perhaps a pound, for which we were to pay one dollar. Making a hole in this lump with a nail, he threaded it with a stout piece of bark, that would serve as a handle to carry or hang it by.

As we had seen no human beings besides each other, for a week, it was natural that we should remain here a short time and talk with people as they came and went from the store. Where they came from was uncertain. They all emerged from the wood surrounding the clearing, and disappeared in a similar manner, no two persons entering the wood at the same place when going away. They came and went like bees from the hive, every man bringing a back-load of some merchantable article, and taking away something in exchange.

Shortly after we had secured our soap, a customer entered the store, and accosted the proprietor, "Have ye got 'ny beeswax here?"

"Yes; what in thunder d'you want of bees-wax?"

"None your darn business what I want it fer. I want beeswax, I do."

"But yer ain't got no gun, and wax is no good ter ye; I don't see what ye want wax fer."

"I want wax fer a sore on my gal's foot. Wax is good 'nough fer any gal's foot."

"Well, how much wax yer want; and how ye goin' to put it on yer wife's foot?"

"When I want yer to help put my gal's foot ter soak in hot wax, I'll ask ye! Gimme a coon-skin's wuth o' wax."

A Mysterious Substance

To my astonishment, the man in charge chiseled the customer off a piece of the same stuff he had sold us for soap. Soon after this, and while I was studying the subject over, and wondering whether we had been sold wax for soap, or if the last buyer had been given soap for wax, still another customer entered, and called for hard-bread and cheese. He was supplied with both, the cheese being chiseled from the same amorphous body that had supplied two other articles. Tightly clinging to the piece we had bought, I determined at the first opportunity to hold an inquest and learn its precise nature.

We remained an hour or more, and I closely watched every customer who entered, hoping to learn more of the subject which was uppermost in my mind. But no one asked for genuine beeswax, creamery cheese or best toilet soap, and I thought it best not to show my ignorance by questioning the proprietor. Dressed as I was, and somewhat grimed and oily, I fancied I would pass for a Texan anywhere. But should I ask such a question as was on my mind, I feared it would "give me away" and in such a case I would be driven crazy by improbable stories of encounters with, and hairbreadth escapes from, tigers, hyenas, snakes and scorpions, the narration of such stories being the conventional way in which sons of Texas amuse a "Boston man."

We saw skunk skins traded for coffee; wild game exchanged for bacon; potatoes bartered for jerked beef, and dog hides swapped for molasses, until I was tired of confusion, and longed for our camp again.

Driving leisurely back we started up a good many goatsuckers, and spent some time in hunting them; but as the thickets were dense, and the birds sharp enough to remain quiet when once hidden, even if almost stepped upon, we secured but two specimens. These birds do not evade capture by flight, but by hiding, and they often escape detection by lying low among the underbrush which they so much resemble in color. A good dog could find them easily, but such game was too insignificant for Absalom to trouble himself with, and he much preferred running a cow or steer over the prairie, to hunting birds.

Absalom on Guard

We had hardly alighted from our wagon, after reaching camp, when Absalom, instead of being pleased to see us, began to growl and bark in a savage manner. He had forgotten our faces, and showing his sharp teeth, defied us to approach the tent. It was in vain that we saluted him by his name, called him "good doggy," or adopted any procedure to show him who we were; he would not allow us to approach him. We tried to knock him out by throwing clubs of wood, but he was a good dodger, and such mode of attack only seemed to make him worse. I was a little afraid he might make a dash at us, for having once felt his teeth, I knew them to be sharp and capable of inflicting a painful wound.

After beating the bush for a half-hour, Mr. Priour became desperate. "Give me my gun," said he, "I'll see if I'm going to be kept from my own camp by that whelp."

"What are you going to do?" I asked.

"What am I going to do?! I'm going to blow that cur back to Corpus Christi!"

I gave him the gun, but hadn't the slightest idea that he would shoot. Taking the weapon in his hand, he turned to me and exclaimed: "You fool! Do you suppose I'm going to kill my dog?!"

I was getting tired myself, and stating the same to my partner, I went into a thick clump of brush down the bluff, and lying upon my face, watched the maneuvers of the opposing forces. I could do no good at camp, and thought it only a question of time when the dog would recognize us.

Mr. Priour walked around and around the tent in a large circle; but whether he went fast or slow, the savage animal kept between him and the goal, all the while showing his gleaming canine teeth and barking vociferously. At last the man went to his wagon, got his harness-lines, and making a noose in them, returned to the vicinity of the dog. Going as near his foe as he cared to, he cast the noose over the animal's head, and then breaking into a run, choked the animal into quietude by dragging him over the rough ground. He then entered the tent hauling the dog behind.

I had a comfortable bed in the brush, and not wishing my partner to know that I had seen the performance, I waited ten or fifteen minutes before going to camp. When I entered the tent, Mr. Priour was smoking and the dog lay at his feet, nearly lifeless from garroting. Saying that I had just awakened from a sound sleep I asked how he had made himself known to the dog. He answered that as soon as I was out of sight, the intelligent animal had come to him of his own accord, and it was I against whom his threats had been so furiously directed. An inquiry as to the cause of the dog's present unconsciousness elicited the opinion that having barked at me so energetically he had completely exhausted himself. My partner evidently was not quite sure that the explanation he offered would prove satisfactory to me; however, he said but little more on the subject, omitting the customary eulogy on the animal's wonderful memory. By daylight on the following morning the dog had recovered his sensibility enough to be about, and exhibited evidences of rapid convalescence.

Our camp here on the bluff of the Aransas River was in a picturesque country. It was a favorite haunt for birds of many species. In places the bluff is cut by deep and narrow fissures. Within these are the homes of many owls who sit drowsily on their back door steps while daylight lasts, patiently waiting for darkness when they sally forth. Woe to the mouse, rat or squirrel which ventures out after dark. Owls will eat small birds, but they much prefer mammals, and a large owl will not hesitate to pounce upon rabbit or skunk. I admire their bravery more than their taste.

We camped on this stream for a week, and found hunting productive; securing fine specimens of great-horned, short-eared, barred and barn owls, and of many other birds—warblers, grosbeaks, night hawks, etc. One morning we saw a column of least terns fishing in the river. They seemed out of place so far from the salt water, but the sight was a pleasing one to us, and we took several of them. From an excavation in the bluff on the far side of the river we took three young barn owls. They were not more than two or three days old, and being too young to stuff, we concluded to make a comfortable bed for them in our wagon, and keep them until they were feathered out. Killing plenty of birds we could easily furnish them enough to eat.

A Chance for a Talk

April 22, we struck our tent, bade farewell to the Aransas River and started on our journey again. During the forenoon the most of our road lay over a barren prairie, but we succeeded in getting a few birds from the *motas* and single trees which occasionally relieved the monotony of prairie travel. In places the ground was much cut up by burrows of the ground squirrel. Like the burrowing owl, these animals have the ability to get out of reach after being killed, but I obtained one specimen in spite of their activity.

About noon we saw a man approaching us on horseback, and as he drew nearer I noticed that he was dragging something by a long rope fastened to the pommel of his saddle. I was about to ask my companion what this could be, when a second thought called to my mind my usual policy upon similar occasions, and I waited to see myself. The man met us just as we neared a *mota*, and according to the customs of the country, we stopped under the trees to exchange ideas and narrate experiences.

People in Texas are never in a hurry; time is long with them, and to meet a person and not stop and talk an hour or two would be considered a breach of prairie etiquette. The gist of the matter in these cases is for each one to find out as much of the other's business as possible, and information to such an end is generally freely given. A conversation between two strangers meeting on the prairie is something like this:

"My name's Bill Goshull; what's yourn?"

"I'm going to Papalote; where are you going?"

"I was born in Webb County, on the Rio Grande; where was you born?"

"I've killed two Mexicans; how many've you killed?"

This talk continues until both parties are satisfied that they have pumped to the bottom, when any other subject is in order.

Dismounting, this man took the object he had been dragging, and placing it near the foot of a tree, seated himself upon it and began to make a cigarette. From a first view, the bundle appeared to resemble more than anything else a dead calf with its hair scraped off. But examining it as well as I was able, without showing my curiosity, I at last discovered beneath dry mud with which it was coated, the letters U. S. M. My sense of inquisitiveness was thus much appeased, and I concluded that this man was one of the much heard of "mail riders." This conclusion Mr. Priour corroborated after the stranger had taken his departure.

A Bird Haunt

At 2 P. M, we reached the town of Refugio, commonly known as "The Mission." Shortly after leaving Refugio we struck the open prairie, where we found buff-breasted and bartramian sandpipers without end. They had not been hunted much, for we took as many as we wished. There being no cows in sight, Absalom condescended to engage himself in our cause, which he did by dashing ahead and scaring any bird he saw us creeping upon. But not being able to work in two places at once, he could hinder only one of us at a time.

At dark we made camp in a growth of weesatche timber, and the ground was nearly destitute of herbage upon which our horses might feed. For this reason Mr. Priour did not fasten the animals at all, but allowed them to go wherever they could find food that would pay for picking. It was my partner's rule to tie one of the horses to some tree at night, but the one so tied often managed to loose himself before morning, and it was no unusual thing for us to spend an hour or two before breakfast looking them up.

The next morning our horses were missing, and we spent the forenoon in hunting for them. They were not found and, having used all of our fresh water the night before we ate at noon a dry meal, as we had done in the morning. While we were eating, a Mexican drove into camp to chat. Mr. Priour had spent several years in Mexico, and spoke the language as fluently as his own. He engaged the visitor to hunt for our lost team, agreeing to pay him four bits should he be successful in his search. An hour later the horses were driven into camp, and we went on our way rejoicing.

We made camp at the St. Nicholas Lakes, which are simply large and shallow depressions, and contain a great deal more mud than water. The next day we tramped through and about these lakes, finding thousands of red-breasted snipe and lesser yellow-legs feeding in them. Had it not been for the density of the shrubbery, this would have proved the finest hunting we had seen. But in spite of all the obstruction, we took as many specimens as we could possibly use. Curlews, stilts, snowy herons, spoonbills, ibes, snow-geese, and ducks of several species made the mud their general feeding ground. Hidden behind their screens of rushes and other vegetation, they saw us long before we came within gunshot of them, and our hunting was rewarded principally by the sight of hundreds of the birds rising *en masse* only to fly a short distance and alight again.

In the few straggling trees about camp we obtained a number of warblers and flycatchers. By an ingenious falsehood of how I had failed to find a bird that I had shot, Mr. Priour called me back of the remains of a large tree, dead long ago. Walking carelessly in the direction he pointed out, I was startled almost to fits by the snarl of an opossum not twelve inches from my legs. Stowed away in a cavity of this large stump, his eyes flashing and his teeth gnashing with rage, he seemed a picture of savageness. Priour laughed heartily at my sudden fright, while I only wondered what had kept the angry animal from flying at and tearing me to pieces.

I wanted to call Absalom and "sic him," but Priour, knowing as well as myself that the dog would run his innocent nose right into the set of tearing ivory, said that he was trying to make a bird hunter of him, and that killing opossums would lead him from his lessons. When I poked the muzzle of my gun into the hollow tree, the animal bit and re-bit it with such fury, that dozens of his teeth snapped like glass, pieces of them flying several feet away from the tree.

Mr. Priour finally put an end to the snarler's life with a charge of shot, and seeming to forget his anxiety abort Absalom's attention being called away from birds, he allowed the dog to play with the 'possum as much as he liked, all the time "sicking him on."

CHAPTER IV
IN WHICH ABSALOM FINDS THE STEW PAN

April 25, we drove to the San Antonio River. The stream was low and not more than fifty or sixty feet in width. On each side was an almost perpendicular bank about sixty yards in length, measured on its surface.

It seemed at first that it would be impossible to drive down the declivity without the wagon sliding over and dropping down ahead of the horses. But Priour was ingenious, and procuring a half cord or less of grape vines from a ravine nearby, he wove them through the wheels so skillfully that they all refused to turn.

The horses were reluctant to step down this hill, and I did not blame them. They'd had experience with such precipitous highways before, and there being no breaching, they well knew what it was to have the wagon crowding their rear.

After a little persuasion, gently punctuated with a switch, the animals gracefully resigned themselves and started down the bank. They knew the situation as well, as anyone could know it, and picked their way as carefully as a human being could have done under similar circumstances, bracing up against the wagon as much as possible.

Everything progressed nicely until about one-third the distance had been made, when one of the grape vines parted. This threw additional strain on another one and it parted also. The wagon crowded harder and harder until the horses could hold the weight against their hips no longer, and, only attempting to keep clear of the heavy wagon, they dashed down the bluff.

Priour heroically clung to the lines, traveling about twelve or fifteen feet at a jump, and it seemed as if the momentum must bury man, wagon and team out of sight in the bank across the stream. But there was an obstacle at the foot of the hill; an abrupt two-foot rise of planking on the edge of the ferry-boat. This obstacle arrested the wagon only, while everything in it fell in a shower on the boat and in the river. Neither Priour nor the horses went off the boat, although they came near doing so.

How I wished Absalom had been on the wagon. My heart bled with regret that he was still on the top of the bank. Such a chance to improve a dog's memory is not often seen, and he knew not what he had missed.

The spilling of our merchandise was no great hardship to us, for on the other side of the river we had to carry everything up to the surface of the earth by hand, the horses having all they could do to get up with the empty wagon.

Such is the typical ferry in Texas. The outlay of a small sum of money would put the way to and from the boat in a passable condition, but as long as a thing is possibly usable here, it is never improved in any manner. About a mile from the ferry and by the side of the river we camped.

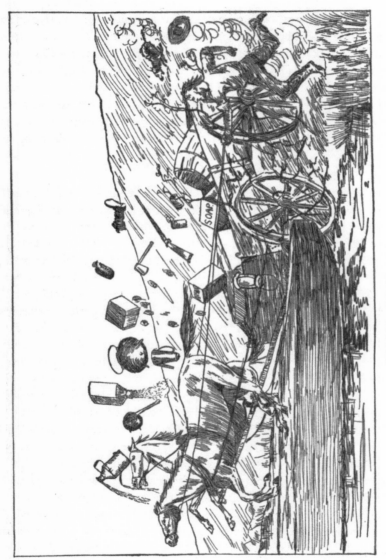

PRIOUR DIVES ABOARD

The San Antonio Bottoms

On this side of the stream there is a strip of heavy timber from one to two miles in width. This growth is known as the "San Antonio Bottoms," and consists of oak, prickly ash, sycamore and pecan. Up and down the stream on each side are small clearings with log cabins, occupied by negroes in countless numbers.

How these people support themselves and their large families, we could not surmise, and they themselves could throw no light on the subject. When I asked one superannuated and white-headed darky, what the people did for a living, he replied: "Peeble roun' he-ar doan do much ob anything, an' doan lib much."

From the number of hungry-looking ones that lazily lounged about our camp, I should say the answer given me was a correct one. They seemed to cultivate very little land, but evidently raised many hogs and children, both of which seemed to swarm the bottoms, and delight in their freedom. The hogs were all branded, and each man could easily know his own at sight. But the hundreds of woolly-headed children had no marks to distinguish one from another, and in case of a taking account of stock in the bottoms, there would be as great confusion with these children as in counting bees from forty hives, and crediting each owner with his proper number.

The negroes flocked about our camp in alarming number, each one followed by a long yellow dog as hungry-looking as his master. The dogs all answered to the same name—Jake. Perhaps it was considered a disgrace to one or the other to have dogs and children answering to the same name, and it seemed as though the community had set the name Jake apart. It was with a feeling of relief that we left the San Antonio River Bottoms Settlement. The country about the Cholette Creek is hilly and uneven, and a tramp along the course of the stream presents a constant change of scene.

The morning after our arrival at the creek, we packed everything in our tent, and prepared to drive to Victoria, seven miles away. Having up to this time lived almost exclusively upon hard-bread and burnt coffee, we were really developing symptoms of scurvy, and prescribed for ourselves a diet of vegetables, to obtain which we would have to visit town.

Absalom was merely the shadow of a dog, and to the best of my recollection had been given nothing edible since leaving Corpus Christi.

Mr. Priour loved the dog, but not enough to feed him, while I hated him just enough to want him to die, and how he maintained his vitality so long was to me a mystery. He had often tried to steal from our stew-pan, but had never succeeded in doing so. He didn't catch any game, for he hadn't sense enough to know what it was until it was dead, skinned, and cooked. He knew just enough to live, and to try and steal, and as far as I at this time believed, he knew no more.

In the care of this dog we were to leave our camp during our absence to Victoria, and fearing he would seize the opportunity to fill his stomach, we endeavored to devise a method by which we could leave our stew-pan of meal and hard-bread where it would be beyond his reach. Several ways were proposed and discussed. We might take the mixture with us, but this would be more trouble than it was worth. The dog was always timid about wetting his feet, and we might carry the food across the stream and hide it, but that was too long a distance to go with it. Finally we hit upon the expedient of putting the food in the fork of a tree near our camp. Drawing the wagon under this tree Mr. Priour stood upon the wheel and placed the dish in the fork of the limbs, fully twelve feet from the ground, and congratulating ourselves that it was out of reach of the guard, we harnessed up our team, and drove to town.

Where They Live on Air and Water

The road from the creek to Victoria is through a farming country, and there having been a drought all through the section almost unprecedented in severity, the crops looked pale and scattering. Everyone was discouraged. Many had planted their seed two and three times before any would start, and we heard bitter complaint of the season from all we met. Stopping at a log cabin to borrow the use of a grindstone, our request was complied with, with the remark, "That grindstun' is the only thing about here the sun ain't wilted yit." It was truly a forsaken-looking place, and we were told that the people and cattle had lived upon air and water for many a day. This last remark threw some light upon the subject of Absalom's existence.

At Victoria we purchased a supply of vegetables which tasted so agreeably to our cracker-tanned palates that we ate of them all the way back to the Cholette, and strewed the road with cabbage stumps and peelings of raw potatoes, beets and onions. The day being a hot one, and the country new to us, we drove very leisurely on our return, stopping every few minutes during the first mile's drive to ask a stranger of his crops, and to hear his tale of woe.

About a mile from the town we reached the open prairie again, and as we repeatedly left our wagon to hunt some rabbit or bird, the time slipped away faster than we realized, and it was late in the afternoon when we reached our camp.

Driving up in front of the tent, the first thing we noted was our sentinel lying on the ground fast asleep. Not only asleep but enormously swollen about the middle. He looked as though he had swallowed a pumpkin, and as wild gourds grew on the prairie, I asked Priour if it was likely that he had swallowed one.

"No, sir," he replied. "Some raccoon has been prowling about the camp, and Absalom has killed and eaten him. I tell you, it's a smart coon that gets ahead of my dog. Bring on yer coons!"

This rhapsody didn't lessen my suspicion in the least, and a few minutes later when we found the empty stew-pan at the foot of the tree in which it had been placed, Priour reluctantly admitted that the animal's turgescence must have been caused by eating meat and hard-bread rather than coons and pumpkins. How the dog had reached the food was at first a puzzle to us, but after carefully examining the tree, and finding the bark gone in places, and prints of his claws in the hard wood, our curiosity was satisfied. That dog could climb a tree as well as a cat.

The meal which had been so adroitly obtained proved to be most too much for a stomach only accustomed to the presence of air and water, and Absalom slept little that night, spending most of the time in moving about from place to place, while he groaned constantly.

One Way to Climb A Tree

The next morning, after a hearty breakfast of vegetables, we took a long tramp up the creek. The growth of annuals in some of the groves was exuberant. Traveling through these masses of weeds, a man shows little more than his head and shoulders, and to a degree reminds an observer of a swimmer struggling in the water. To rest himself and look about, a swimming man will climb any rock or snag that chances to be in his way, and while working our way through these mazy botanical gardens we invariably climbed every fallen log we saw, and took a look about us. We drove up a good many goatsuckers, and killed several of them. Mourning warblers were quite abundant, and flitted about the undergrowth with such rapidity that they seemed to appear and disappear like flashes of lightning. Indeed, we did not recognize these birds as mourning warblers until after repeated failures we had succeeded in securing one. Up to this time we had never taken any, and being anxious to obtain a few, we spent several hours shooting at streaks, and were rewarded by some half dozen specimens.

Mr. Priour discovered the nest of a swallow-tailed kite in the extreme top of a tall cottonwood tree, and having brought the harness lines with him to use in such a case, he made arrangements to climb to the nest. The lower limb was about twenty feet from the ground, and after several unsuccessful attempts, one end of the line was thrown over this branch. Fastening one end of the rope to his foot, and keeping himself rigidly erect, we attempted to elevate him to the arm-like extension above, by the combined effort of his hands and my own, on the other part of the line. For a short time everything worked nicely, and our mechanical ingenuity was apparently about to result in his reaching the limb. But he was too sanguine. When within about two feet of the limb he let go of the line we were both hauling on, and made an effort to grasp the branch. His dexterity was not equal to the occasion, and as a result of his hasty movement his center of gravity went through a series of alterations, and finally left the man hanging by one foot, and swinging like a pendulum in mid-air. Having the other end of the line wound several times around my wrists, the sudden and unexpected strain nearly took me off my feet. Since I was considerably heavier than Mr. Priour, I held my own against his weight.

In an instant the thought came into my mind that the proper thing to do under the circumstances would be to fasten my end of the rope to a bush or tree, find a long stick with diverging branches at the end, and try to restore the man to his former position by catching his neck between the branches, and exerting my strength on the other end of the pole. But before I could arrive at a decision in regard to the proper course to pursue, he had begun to clamor: "Loose away! Loose away!"

Being somewhat excited and anxious to comply with his demands, I hastily freed the line from my hands, and with a dull thud the man dropped to the ground. Mr. Priour was not discouraged by his failure, and after scraping the dirt and leaves out of his hair, was as ready to renew the task as he had been to begin it. This time he was more methodical, and made no attempt to grasp the branch until he was within easy reach of it. Standing upon this limb, which was at right angles to the trunk, and steadying himself with one hand against the tree, he cast the line over another limb still higher up, and hoisted himself to it without my assistance. The line was not long enough to reach from this branch to the ground.

After a deal of hard labor he secured the nest, and although he left pieces of clothing and skin in various parts of the tree, he stowed in his hat and brought safely to the ground a fine set of kite's eggs, which he thought fully repaid him for all his labor. We also obtained here two fine specimens of adult kites.

Mr. Priour Weeps For His Pet

Following the course of the stream on our return we found many birds wading and feeding therein. Snowy, little blue and white herons were scattered along the creek, and we obtained specimens of each of these beautiful birds, which at this time of the year are in their breeding plumage, and look their prettiest. Snake-birds were numerous both on the stream and on the trees by the bank, but we had no wish to kill them.

Our pet barn owls, which had traveled with us since the 21st of April, had grown rapidly, and as they had begun to take on a yellow color to their feathers, we decided to kill and stuff them. It was with great reluctance that I took the life of my two, George and Jabez. Mr. Priour wept like a child when he thought of killing his own pet, May. But their sufferings were of short duration, and cotton was soon substituted for their own natural skin-filling.

CHAPTER V
THE EPISODE OF THE SOAP

Although camped in a lovely spot, we were not without trials. An old sow and a litter of six pigs lived in the vicinity, and their chief object seemed to be to annoy us as much as was in their power. They had found the many bodies of birds that we threw out in the brush, and not being satisfied with the abundance of food thus furnished them, they came into our tent as often as we could drive them out. They would crawl under the sides so quietly that we would only know of their presence by the grunt of satisfaction that no hog or pig can refrain from producing when he finds something that pleases his appetite, and such a sound to us always meant another bird gone to the pigs.

These young animals could most successfully dodge a lantern or coffee pot, and I believe I never succeeded in hitting one of them in the daytime. They were private property, belonging to the owner of the pasture in which we had camped, otherwise we would have made soup of them after their first invasion. It was in vain that we strove to make Absalom an enemy of the swine. He had made their acquaintance upon our arrival, and would fondle and caress the pigs at every visit they made us. Indeed, I was not certain that he did not obtain a part of his sustenance from the same source, and in common with the young pigs. He could easily have worked this imposition on the old sow, for to his very caudal append-age he resembled a pig as much as a dog.

The conduct of Absalom aroused Mr. Priour's anger, and on several occasions when we had returned from hunting and found the pigs in the tent, and the dog lounging indifferently about camp, he had beaten the animal whose sole duty should have been to guard our treasures. But his master's exertions were in vain. Finally Mr. Priour gave up beating him, and whenever I fumed at the dog because he had lain quiet and allowed a pig to stand upon his back in order to reach some of our birds, the man would say: "Poor dog. He's just so dog-on'd tired from hunting he can't move."

Pigs in the Tent at Midnight

Priour had repented of the anger which prompted him to try punishment on the animal, but I was not so forgiving. I was constantly annoyed by the pigs, but felt much more like killing the dog than the swine. I was strongly tempted to entice the canine away from camp, and send a charge of shot into his empty skull. But for the fear of making his master my mortal enemy, I should certainly have done this job.

One night about twelve o'clock I awoke from a sound sleep and found the whole family of swine inside the tent. They had evidently been there an hour or more working destruction to everything within reach, and as usual, Absalom had kindly allowed himself to be used as a stepladder. Some were eating hard-bread, others crunching potatoes and cabbages. They were devouring everything. Plaster, arsenic, cotton, powder and shot were all fast disappearing. They had found our bird skins and were rapidly tearing them to pieces. The old sow had rooted Mr. Priour off his blanket, and shoved him fully halfway out of the tent, and still he slept. Jumping to my feet I seized my gun, and using it as a club fought right and left.

> Pigs to the right of me,
> Pigs to the left of me,
> Pigs in front of me,
> Squealed and scampered.

My first blow fell upon Absalom's head, and with a howl of pain he shot out under the ragged curtain. I showered blows upon the pigs until the tent was occupied only by myself with one-half of my partner.

Lighting again our lantern which had been extinguished, I made a hasty examination of the surroundings. Our camp had been most thoroughly sacked, and the sight was a sickening one. My partner was so covered with plaster and arsenic that he seemed to have been dipped into a flour barrel, and would have passed for a spook. Nearly everything in the tent bore evidence of an encounter with either tooth, nose or foot, and I thought it best not to make any attempt at cleaning up until daylight.

Mr. Priour was sleeping so sweetly, it seemed a pity to wake him, and smoothing out my blanket I lay down again. But I could not sleep; my thoughts were upon my companion, and I asked myself the question: "Suppose the pigs should eat that portion of the man that was outside, who would care for the widow and orphans?" I grasped his feet and dragged him within the tent again, then, feeling that I had done my duty, I went to sleep.

Absalom Bears Scars of Conflict

Early in the morning I took a look outside. Absalom was lying near the tent, a large swelling on his face showed me the exact spot where I had struck him with the butt of the gun, and I was thankful that he had not the power of speech to tell his master how he had received the injury.

The pigs were nowhere in sight; they were likely engaged in digesting their food, and sleeping off the effects of their midnight banquet. I hoped they had all eaten enough arsenic to kill them, but swine, as is well known, are not easily killed by that poison, and I looked for their reappearance before noon.

Gathering some brush and leaves I was about to build a fire and get breakfast, when I heard articulations from within the tent. A stranger hearing these sounds

I RESORT TO ARMS

might have supposed them to be from some caged lion, but it was Priour. He had waked up. He had found things somewhat stirred up inside, and was expressing his thoughts. Poking out his head he said: "I'd like to know what's been going on inside here! Who turned arsenic all over my clothes, and rubbed feathers into my ears?"

"I don't know," I replied. "Perhaps Absalom had a fit during the night, and scattered things about; I see there is a bruise on his face where he must have struck a box or something."

"No, sir," he answered. "My dog don't have fits. That bruise he got yesterday killing coons. I saw him when he struck his head against a tree. I tell you what, I dreamed last night that pigs were in the tent, and dog-on'd if they ain't been here, too."

"Do you suppose Absalom would let pigs in during the night?" I asked.

"Well, now, if your face was swelled up like his was when he turned in, I guess you'd let most anything in. I tell you, if 'twasn't for that dog, we'd been eat up long ago. That coon he killed last night smelt our cabbage, and was steering right for the tent."

"I have never seen him kill a coon," I said.

"That's no reason he don't kill them; I don't expect we know half he kills and drags off into the brush. That bunch on his head he can well feel proud of, for he got it in fair fight, and in defending this camp, too."

After consuming a breakfast of what the pigs in their haste had left for us, we went about clearing up after the rape of the camp. Finding one of his choicest skins conspicuously minus the head, Priour exclaimed: "Now, I'll be dog-on'd if I ain't going to kill them hogs if I get hung for it. I won't be trifled with in any such way."

"Good," said I. "You kill the pigs and I'll kill Absalom; I'd rather have coons in the camp than swine. Our blankets look as though they had been in a hog pen for a week."

"You let Absalom be. He's doing his best for us, and he'll die yet defending this camp if we don't get out of here soon, I'd rather sleep on a hog blanket than to have my ears chewed off by coons. What'd we done in the live oaks if 'twasn't for that dog? Wasn't we hedged in by skunks, and didn't he keep them off? The only reason that first one got in was because we tied the poor animal to the wagon, and he couldn't get away. I noticed there didn't any skunks fool around the wagon that night."

Taking down our tent and dragging it away, so that we could better see our possessions, we worked patiently until near noon, Priour constantly raving about the swine, while I as constantly condemned the dog.

An Adventure with a Cake of Soap

In rearranging our property I came across the cake of soap which we had bought at Papalote, and which I had not thought of since leaving camp on the Aransas River. The pigs had eaten nearly half of this substance, and I determined to try the remainder of it for washing purposes.

Taking the soap in my hand I walked to the creek, and prepared to shampoo my head. The soap-like substance was odorless and not very soluble, but after soaking it in the water a short time, it felt a little moist, and I rubbed it thoroughly into my hair, now quite long.

After having, as I supposed, insinuated a sufficient quantity into my flowing locks, I attempted to lay the material upon the ground, but it stuck fast to my plumage. I labored diligently and tried my utmost to liberate my head from the sticky mass, and as a last resort was obliged to take my pocket knife, and cut all the hair between the soap and my head. I then tried to wash away what had stuck to my hair, but it was as useless as to try to wash off pitch, and I was thankful when, after a severe exertion, I had succeeded in freeing my hand from my occiput.

I had to spend a half-hour rubbing my hands in the sand before I could take hold of anything and let go again; and if this was a fair sample of Texas soap, I felt that a thorough washing once a year would be often enough for anyone. Harpooning with a sharp stick the piece that I had cut from my head, and pulling out the tufts of hair clinging to it, I returned to camp.

Mr. Priour was getting ready to go to the creek and take a wash himself. "How's that soap for washing?" he asked, for, like myself, he had never seen anything like it before.

"Fine," I replied. "I don't care whether you call it soap, cheese, glue or scrap-iron. It's the best thing to remove dirt that I have ever seen, and I wish I had bought another dollar's worth to take home with me and show the people that Texas is far ahead of New England in the soap line."

Mr. Priour's face assumed a pleased expression at my compliment to the State of which he was a native, and taking the soap by the handle I had left in it, he proceeded to the creek. I watched him until the brush hid him from view, and felt just a little guilty at the false report I had made concerning the soap, for I knew from what he had previously said that he would use it on his head before trying it elsewhere. I imagined myself as cruel and heartless as the uncle in *Babes in the Woods*, who smiled upon his brother's children just before sending them away to die, and I repented almost to the point of running after the man and correcting my statements. But he was now out of sight and hearing, and I thought he could not well get stuck up worse than I had been, and I let him go.

Mr. Priour in Distress

During his absence I took a stroll with my gun and killed a barred owl from the top of a cottonwood tree. The top of this tree was thickly set with short branches, and my owl caught fast in this network of twigs. Going back to camp I procured the harness lines, and by their help reached my bird. The place in which it had lodged was such an almost impenetrable tangle of branches, that I tore my clothing in many places, and after I had descended to the ground I found that I had left a large piece of my overalls among the highest branches. I thought little of my loss, and hearing my partner shout, I picked up my bird, shouldered my gun and hurried back to camp.

Mr. Priour was there. His hands were stuck fast in his hair, and as he had removed his coat and shirt before wrestling with the soap, the upper part of his body was entirely nude.

"Where's your shirt?" I asked.

"Where's my shirt?! Down by the creek, you fool, and to keep my pants from coming off, I've had to walk bow-legged all the way up here! Get that ax and cut off my head or my hands, I don't care which. Some cuss'll come along and carry off my gun if I don't get back to the creek pretty soon."

"Did you see any mermaids in the creek?" I asked.

"No, you fool. Do you suppose I'd come to camp this way if I'd seen a mermaid? I'd rubbed the dog-on'd stuff all over her."

Conducting the man to a tree, and backing him up against it, with the ax I chopped him from his fetters. He then asked me why I had deceived him in regard to the character of the soap. I told him that I had had no difficulty with it, and that he must have struck an imperfection that was not uncovered when I had made use of it.

This answer satisfied him to a certain extent, and calling Absalom to him, he cleaned his hands as best he could by rubbing them the whole length of the animal, ears and tail included. But he took from the poor dog about as much hair as he gave him pitch in return, and I thought if Absalom should attempt to scratch himself against a tree, he too, would have to be chopped out. Having his hands free again, my partner hurried away to get his shirt and gun.

Although we had had such a serious time with the soap, I thought our experience must have been a good deal less trying than if we had bought the stuff for cheese.

I thought of the family of the man who had bought cheese at Papalote on the day we were there, and I could picture them seated around their humble board, all anxious for a bite of the infrequent food which the loving husband and father had procured at the expense of a pint of buzzard oil. In my imagination I could see some wee tot's face, all aglow with pleasing expectancy as she said: "Papa, papa, I want teese."

Poor child. How her little heart would ache from the keen disappointment in store for her. I pitied her. That sweet innocent mouth bedaubed with such sticky stuff. I felt like howling to the Papalote merchant: "If you didn't have cheese, why didn't you say so! If you had never seen any soap, why didn't you own up to it like a man, and not be the cause of men losing their hair and scalp, and babes their tongue and teeth!" But the man who had bought the substance for something edible was broad-shouldered and well-built, and I fancied that on the day following his tussle with the sticky compound, the groceryman might need to be pitied most of all.

A Rare Bird Up a Tree

Seating myself upon an old log near our camp, I skinned and stuffed my barred owl. Priour had reached the creek in time to get ahead of any "cuss" after his gun, and down in the depth of the grove I heard him shooting rapidly. Thinking he had come across a flock of warblers, and was going to get a dozen or two, I at first paid little attention to the continued banging, but as it continued without abatement I was curious to know its meaning, not knowing if he was in trouble, and was firing as a signal for me to come to his rescue. Going rapidly in the direction of the sound I soon found him, directly under the tree from which a short time before I had taken my owl. The piece of cloth from my overalls, which I had left in the tree, was still there, and it was at this that Mr. Priour was sending charge after charge of No. 4 shot. Without desisting from firing he informed me that there was a bird in that tree not described in any book, and that it was so protected by vines that the shot didn't seem to reach it, but he was going to have it if it took the last charge of powder and shot he possessed to bore a hole to it through the briers.

From where I was standing I could see this object very plainly, and as it fluttered back and forth with the wind, it did resemble a living thing. I had often been deceived in a like manner myself, for very often a bird almost hidden from view in a tangle of twigs and branches will only show its whereabouts by the slightest visible movement. Many a charge of shot have I sent after a bunch of feathers, a piece of moss, or the remains of a dilapidated nest, and as Priour always laughed at me on such occasions, I was glad at last to see him deceived likewise. I should not have mourned the loss of my whole suit, if by leaving it in a treetop I could have sold my partner, for I was tired of such questions as: "What you going to do with that snarl of grass you killed this morning?" "You've killed that bunch of briers, now why don't you climb the tree and get it?" Wishing the man good luck in his undertaking I returned to camp.

He Does Not Bring the Bird

Ten or fifteen minutes later Mr. Priour came for his harness lines, stating that he had killed the bird, and was going back to get it. I wondered what he would say upon his return.

I thought if I were in his place I should be likely to report that during my absence from the tree a hawk had come and carried away the prize. But Priour would know the source of the piece of cloth as soon as he reached it, and I was anxious for his arrival at camp with some explanation or excuse for his fierce attack upon an inanimate thing.

It was now getting late, and I made coffee, and cooked as good a supper as possible with our supply of provisions, for I thought Priour could find some solace in filling his stomach. I expected the man every minute. I knew he had had plenty of time to climb the tree, and reach camp while I was getting ready our fare.

An hour passed. It was now quite dark and I was somewhat anxious, and thinking the man might have met with some accident in climbing the tree, I went into the timber to look for him. But everything about the scene of the heavy cannonading was as quiet as death, and satisfying myself that the man was not in the near vicinity, I returned to camp, knowing that a search for him in the darkness would be vain. Building a large and bright campfire I seated myself by it, and smoked my pipe.

It was a dark night, and my range of vision extended only a short distance from the blazing pile which was just far enough from the timber to outline indistinctly the tall trees, which stood about like so many motionless sentinels. Absalom I supposed to be with his master.

I could hear an occasional squeal and grunt from the pigs which had made their headquarters near our own. These being the only sounds that came to my ears, they were rather agreeable than otherwise—much more agreeable than when the animals were ravaging our stores. Having smoked to my satisfaction, and tired of sitting by the fire without company, I crept into the tent and was soon asleep.

CHAPTER VI
THE RETURN OF THE MISSING

I had camped long enough in Texas to know that a man was liable to have his sleep disturbed at almost any time. By spending eight nights out of every ten in the open air for years, a man may accustom himself to the tolerance of all kinds of noise, and all sensations short of severe pain; but I hadn't camped out long enough for that, and when Mr. Priour came creeping back to camp at about midnight, I was fully aware of his proximity before he entered the tent. Keeping perfectly quiet and feigning sleep I waited for his entrance.

Going to the dying fire he mended it, and by its light appeased his hunger with the stew that I had left for him. He then came to the tent and carefully pulling back the fold of cloth at the entrance, peered in, and satisfying himself that I was unconscious, he noiselessly stepped over me and crawled into his blanket. He said nothing to me nor I to him, and we were both soon asleep.

Tells a Straight Story

The next morning Mr. Priour was an entirely different person from what he had been on the day before. His loquacity had entirely disappeared and his face bore an expression of general dissatisfaction. I asked him no questions about the heavy firing, but he volunteered a story himself.

He said that he had reached the bird, that it was different from any he had ever seen, but so torn in pieces by the shot as to be worthless, and he was going to try and get its mate, which he had seen flying about the same tree.

As he had broached the subject, I thought it safe to say something myself. "Did you have much trouble in climbing the tree?" I asked.

"No, not very much. I saw a piece of your overalls about six feet above where my bird was killed. Did you climb that tree?"

"Yes; I climbed it to get an owl I had killed in its very top; and by the way, what kept you out so late last night?"

"Oh, I was hunting for Absalom. He's gone somewhere. I haven't seen him since four o'clock yesterday."

Mr. Priour told such a straight story that I could hardly discredit it, but I couldn't quite believe that he would spend half a night tramping through that dark grove looking for his dog, neither could I think he wasn't deceived by the piece of clothing which I had left in the tree. But I said nothing of my doubts.

Priour's horses were trained for stalking. Screened by one of them, it was an easy matter to approach any game, even on the open prairie. Wild geese and ducks, and many other birds seem greatly to fear the presence of man, but they will allow a horse to approach within a few yards of them, never thinking that there might be a man and gun concealed by the harmless quadruped. I have seen my partner stalking behind his horse go within easy range of a flock of geese or ducks, and kill fifteen or twenty of them at a single shot.

Taking one of these horses I rode several miles up the creek. There was some game about the water, and by using my horse as described I had little difficulty in getting a half-dozen of them. The sky was cloudy and a fine mist was beginning to fall, and I returned to camp, reaching there just as my partner was packing things in the tent in anticipation of a rainstorm.

A Ferocious Canine

Absalom had not yet returned, and Priour asked me if I had seen anything of him during my ride up the creek.

He mused awhile and finally exclaimed: "I know where that dog is; he's at the San Antonio River."

"How do you know he is there?"

"I know dog-on'd well he is. Some coon has followed us and stole him, and I'm going to ride back there tomorrow, and kill every nigger in the bottoms!"

"The dog may show up before morning."

"Well, if he don't show up I'll spill enough black blood to drown every yeller cur they've got up there, whether they stole Absalom or not. If they didn't steal him, 'twa'n't because they didn't want him. They're just too dog-on'd lazy to come after him, that's all. Too poor to keep a horse, and too lazy to travel that distance afoot. Why, they wouldn't walk out here for a thousand-dollar dog; and have it brought to them besides, without their ever stirring a step for it."

"If they are as lazy as that, I don't think they would come after your dog, and besides, they have plenty of their own just like him," I said.

"No; they haven't plenty just like him! There ain't a decent dog in the whole bottoms settlement. My dog wouldn't be there two hours, before he'd kill the last one of them curs, and drag their carcasses into the river, and be ready to commence on the niggers next. My dog would ruin the whole village, and they all know it, too. Didn't you see him tackle one of them when we were there?"

"No, I didn't see it; I thought the dog was in the tent all the time."

"Well, he wa'n't. He stripped one man's hide from his shoulder to the ground. They were all glad enough to see us leaving. Half of them didn't dare to come down out of the trees while we were there, and if I'd known Absalom could climb as well as he does, I'd sent him up after them."

"If they are as afraid of the dog as that, I shouldn't think they'd steal him any quicker than a dove would steal a henhawk."

"You can bet they wouldn't. They'd as soon think of sending one of their young ones into the river to steal a sixteen-foot alligator as to look that dog in the face."

Mr. Priour had given vent to his feelings, and appeared to feel much the better for expressing his opinion of the San Antonio negroes. He hadn't shown any particular signs of hatred toward these people during our stay in their vicinity, and I concluded that the loss of his dog was responsible for his sudden feeling of contempt for them — "whether they stole the animal or not."

In the afternoon it rained in torrents. This was the first rainfall we had had since leaving Corpus Christi, and we had a fine opportunity to test the protecting qualities of our tent. I believe that at first some of the rain falling upon our cover did run down the outside, but the rapidly falling water soon filled the meshes of the composite structure to complete saturation, when it lost its distinction as a tent, and became a huge colander dripping in a hundred places.

As each stream of drops assumed the color of the material through which it filtered, the inside of the tent reminded me of a beautiful kaleidoscopic picture. We had green drops from a cambric curtain, yellow drops from overalls, red drops from a petticoat, chocolate drops from a dirty blanket, besides blue drops, white drops, black drops, and mixed drops *ad infinitum*.

We had our hands full of business, being constantly engaged in moving our boxes and bedding about, trying to find places where they would not get too gaudily painted. The purest spot of all we found directly under the breech between a catskin and boot-leg, which opening admitted only undefiled rain water. The dampness of the ground called out the scorpions, and they became exceedingly thick about our camp. Traveling back and forth through the wet grass on the edge of the grove they seemed to me to be hunting for something to sting, and I kept out of their way as much as possible. Toward night the rain ceased falling, and the atmosphere seemed much clearer than it had been for several days.

Perhaps a Pterodactyle?

It was an invigorating pleasure to breathe the bracing air, and the grove became filled with music from the throats of a thousand warblers, all singing thanks for the refreshing shower. Hundreds of bats made their appearance, and darted to and fro in the edge of the grove as thankful as their feathered neighbors. Kites and night-hawks came from their retreats, and had their fill of the many insects, which seemed to have been called into new life by the change of air.

The trees in the grove were dripping, and to walk through the weeds would seem more like wading for shellfish than hunting for birds; so we thought the remainder of the day could be most profitably spent in shaking out our bird skins and cleaning them of their many-colored spots of dye. Some of the coloring matter which had been manufactured in the meshes of our tent left a permanent stain, and we found that we really had "specimens concerning which no book had ever offered a description." It was somewhat discouraging to find so many of our trophies ruined by the rain, but birds were plenty, and we thought we could replace most of them.

About dark we saw some object approaching us from the direction of the creek. It was moving slowly and apparently with great effort. From our position near the tent we studied the appearance and gait of this oscillating body which was so clumsily nearing us, and tried to decide whether it was a huge tortoise or a devil-fish. "Well, I'll be dog-on'd," said Priour. "I've traveled over every square foot of this State and I never saw anything like that before. What kind of a critter call that be; I'll have his hide and make a stew of his liver whatever it is," and he reached for his rifle.

The object drew nearer and nearer, and we could see that there were projections from its sides and after part-projections somewhat suggestive of crippled wings in front, and a dragging parachute behind.

"Isn't that a pterodactyle?" I asked of my partner.

"No, sir; it's no pterodactyle. Pterodactyles don't have that style of motion. They can travel faster than a nigger run by bees; and what's more, did you ever see a pterodactyle so far from the salt water?"

"I never saw one anywhere. That animal's near enough to shoot now, why don't you do it?"

Absalom as a Collector

My words were lost, for with an enthusiastic spasm of joy my comrade made a dash forward and embraced the object in his arms. Peeling the leaves, grass, brush and bark away he at last reached the nucleus—Absalom. Poor buzzard, he had evidently had a serious time with the soap Priour had rubbed into him, while trying to clean his own hands.

Probably the dog had tried to clean himself by rolling among the underbrush until he had incased himself in a straightjacket; and it was surprising what an amount of vines and briers he had been able to drag about.

The return of the missing dog filled his master's heart with ecstasy. He at once reassumed his wonted mirthfulness, and not even reminiscences of the "undescribed specimen" interfered with his glee.

"I tell you," he said, "I knew that was Absalom as soon as I saw him; I knew he wouldn't be away from this camp another night, if he had to drag out the bottom of the creek to get here."

"If you knew it was Absalom, what did you get your rifle for?" I asked.

"To clean it, of course. Wa'n't it under all them waterspouts in the tent? I take care of my rifle if I don't do anything else. I hope you don't think I didn't know my own dog."

"I didn't know if you had been deceived by the cocoon he had spun about him." "No, sir, no cocoon has the memory of that dog. He does beat all, coming back to camp all alone and bringing specimens, too. I found the prettiest set of vulture's eggs wrapped up on his back you ever saw. He'd found them and remembered his master."

"I didn't know the dog was an egg hunter."

"Well, he is; I've known him to crack open a turtle shell as big as your hat, and dig out the eggs and bring to me."

Finding that Priour could do nothing but sing the praises of Absalom, I left him with the dog, while I cooked our supper. The next day we made preparations to continue our journey. We had been on this creek nine days, and had been successful in obtaining variety as well as quantity of skins; but the specimens secured were mostly of small birds, wrens, flycatchers and warblers. Of the latter we found many different species—Kentucky, black-and-white, prothonotary, blue-winged, parula, yellow, chestnut-sided, Blackburnian, black-throated, hooded, pine, Maryland yellow throat, Canadian and mourning warblers.

CHAPTER VII
PLOUGHING A STRAIGHT FURROW

May 6 we packed our wagon and pulled away from the Cholette Creek. Late in the afternoon we arrived in Victoria, and as we were to buy provisions and ship our birds from this place, we camped for the night in a vacant lot. In the morning we shipped our bird skins and purchased at the Victoria National Bank a supply of coffee and crackers.

We didn't eat crackers because we liked them, but because of their convenience in carrying. They were always ready to be eaten, and as neither Priour nor myself would stoop to do any more cooking than the conditions demanded, we ate crackers three times a day, excepting once in a week or so, when we would cook some game or meal.

At early daylight we were astir, and after eating breakfast and packing anew our wagon we prepared to bid an *adieu* to the town. We inquired of the road to Texana, but no one seemed to be able to show us where it was. They could all point in the direction of the town, and tell us to travel that way, but as we knew the direction ourselves, their information was not very helpful.

"Texana's About That Range"

Taking a road that seemed to be leading east from Victoria, we drove out a mile or more, when the path we had followed gradually curved around and led us back in the direction we had come. During this drive we saw no point at which we could leave the path, and we were soon back in town again. We took another road which seemed to lead our way, but when we had reached the suburbs, it too, curved around and pointed back to the point we had left thirty minutes before.

Mr. Priour now became angry. We had driven several miles, and were no nearer the road to Texana than when at camp. "Now, I tell you I'm going to Texana," he said.

"How are you going if you don't know the road? Hadn't we better wait a short time and make more inquiries? People are not up yet."

"I'll show you how I can get out of this place whether there's any road or not! I've drove through swamps that never heard of a road. You see that tree off there on the prairie? Well, I should say Texana's about that range, and I'm going straight for that tree. I'm from Corpus Christi! G'long there."

Mr. Priour was in earnest, and, wheeling the team about, he drove in the direction mentioned. The first obstacle we met was a low bush fence. The horses were urged through this, and we crossed a small garden to a rail fence on the other side. This was easily knocked down, and we left the garden to trespass on still other private grounds. Most people were yet in bed, and we met with no interference during our rude egress from the settlement. We drove through back yards, sheep pens and cornfields, over gulleys, dikes, wood piles and door steps until we were clear of all signs of civilization.

Once on the open prairie we increased our speed, and when about three miles from town struck a road that appeared to lead in our way. This we supposed was from Victoria to our next harbor, and such it proved to be. About dark our camp was approached by a man leading a horse by the bridle. They both looked tired and the poor animal was so weak that he seemed ready to fall. The man stated that he had been on the road to Victoria for several days, but on account of the scarcity of grass, his horse had played out, and he had led him all that day. Both were hungry, and we welcomed them to the hospitality of our modest fare. The man thanked us heartily for his repast; but in the eyes of the dumb beast as he crunched his corn, I could read a volume of thanks inexpressible by human tongue.

Early on the following morning we were up and about, and furnishing our visitors with a substantial breakfast, saw them off for Victoria, the man leading his horse as before. The distance before them was but eighteen miles, and we thought they could easily make it before night.

Our road this day lay over the same barren soil as upon the previous one, and the drive was monotonous and uninteresting. About noon we reached Texana, and crossing the stream on the bank of which is the town, we came to camp.

CHAPTER VIII
RUNNING DOWN SOMETHING ALIVE

Goldsmith's "Sweet Auburn" is Texana. This place contains the ruins of twelve or fifteen houses; some only slightly out of repair—a door or window gone—others ready to fall at any moment, and still others in a state of collapse. We took a stroll through the forsaken streets, and entered nearly every building. All were unoccupied, and our voices echoed and re-echoed through the rooms with such a hollow, distressing sound, that we unconsciously refrained from talking while within them.

We examined every house, shed and hen-coop; explored every street, alley and dooryard, but not a sign of life could we find about the place.

"Now, I'll be dog-on'd," said my partner. "This is the deadest town I've struck yet. Here's houses enough for forty. I'd like to see some soul stirring about, if 'twa'n't more 'n a dog."

"Why are you so anxious to see somebody?"

"I want to see something with life in it, and if I caught glimpse of a man I'd run him down if it took a week. What's that?!"

"What's what?" I asked.

"I seen a pair of nigger heels flip around the corner of that shed there. Hey, you black devil! Come out of there!"

Priour dashed off in the direction he had pointed out, and I soon saw a negro rush up one of the streets, followed closely by my comrade who continually shouted: "Hold up! Hold up there! Head him off! Head him off, you fool!"

The race was an exciting one—across streets, through sheds, over wood-piles, under fences, and around houses. Absalom kindly lent his assistance in the chase, and following close to his master's heels, he occasionally stopped barking, long enough to seize the pair of legs in front of him, and strip off a piece of breeches.

The dog knew something was up, but didn't seem to know what nor whom to assail; and being better acquainted with his master than with the negro, he vented his rage upon the former.

This was displeasing to Priour, and several times when almost within grabbing distance of the runaway, he had to stop and administer a kick or two to the animal who possessed such a "wonderful memory." This punishment had only a temporary effect, and the intelligent canine would soon be as interested in the charge as before. The negro was running as for his life, and as I saw him enter a building which had no visible opening save the one where he had gone in, I believed the chase to be at an end. But not so. The fugitive was a butter, and as Priour entered the opening, the negro's head crashed through the other side of the house, and mid the flying boards and shingles he made his exit into the world again. Priour soon followed by the same butted opening, and the running contest was in order again.

Wanted to Converse

I made it my business to move about just enough to keep the men in sight, and several times I wished myself on the top of some chimney, where I could have an unobstructed view of the struggle. I had no interest at stake on the result, and I didn't care to "head him off." I was too much afraid of that head to try and intercept it, for I had already seen what it was capable of going through.

In the end Priour proved to be the better runner, and after the fleeing negro had carried away several sections of rail fence, lost his hat and shoes, and hung his clothing in various places about the town, he was my partner's captive. Both were now panting for breath, and as I approached they seated themselves face to face upon a pile of boards.

I hadn't the slightest idea of what Mr. Priour's object could be in chasing the man, but supposed it to be some sudden fancy that had possessed him to do such a thing.

"Why didn't you head him off?" were the words that first greeted me.

"What do you want that man for?" I asked. "Didn't you know there was a law against kidnapping?"

"Now, this here ain't no kid. He's a black goat, and there's no law in Texas against goat nabbing. I want to know about this town!" and addressing the negro he continued: "Where's all the folks that live about here? What've you done with them?"

"Dey no be here any mo'. Dey dun gone up de kreak."

"What'd they go up the creek for, you hound?"

"De houses all dun blown down, massa, an' de county seat kerred up dar, too."

"Why didn't you stop when I told you to?"

"Good Lawd, I neber seed de likes. I thought you chicken thief. Lem me go, an' I neber do dis scrape agin."

"Well, the next time I tell you to stop, you stop! I'm from Corpus Christi!"

"Yes, sar. I knowed you's from Corpus Christi—no man roun' here run like dat. Dis nigger hab long feet, but he no git ahead ob Corpus Christi man. I dun stop next time, boss, sho!"

"Well, it's the best thing for you to do. I never run a nigger yet but what I caught him, and I'd had you if I'd had to sweat myself down to twenty pounds to do it."

"Has yer got a chaw terbacker, boss?" asked the steaming negro in front of me. I furnished him with a "chaw," for I thought he had earned it. I knew that the blessed herb would relieve the sense of fatigue better than anything else in the world.

WANTS TO TALK TO HIM

Turning to my partner I said: "Now you've pumped your man and are satisfied about the emptiness of these houses, let's go to camp and have some dinner, I'm hungry."

At the word 'dinner', the negro's eyes snapped like a parlor match, for the sound seemed to bring to his mind recollections of hoe-cakes and onions long gone by, and I thought it might now be his turn to pursue us to our camp. I invited him to come with us, and he eagerly accepted.

An Appetite Unappeasable

Trotting briskly about the place he quickly gathered the fragments of his clothing hanging about on posts and fences, and followed us across the stream. Here we prepared to put away a liberal supply of hard-bread and coffee.

Thinking to apologize for the quality of our fare I said: "These crackers are old and somewhat hard, but are the best we have; I hope you can eat them."

"Oh, good golly! I eats anything a hog can swaller, and hab got big mouf, too— look—Ya! ya! ya! I's a African."

"Ha! ha! ha!" laughed Priour. "I guess you haven't seen many of them in your life. Why, this black elephant'd eat you and me both, boots and all if he dared to, and then go for the dog. I'll bet a hog-skin he ain't had a taste of anything fit to eat for a month. I've seen black niggers, white niggers, and yellow niggers, and they're always the same animal—always looking for something to eat, and never finding enough."

"'Deed dat's true," chimed the grinning subject. "What dese Corpus Christi men doan know ain no 'count, and 'pears to me I neber did git 'nough to eat yit."

The negro's appetite was truly amazing. His stomach must have extended into his long heels, for he ate and ate until everything about him had disappeared, and he then looked wistfully about as if in search of a ham-bone.

I thought that Mr. Priour might be offended at my asking the man to dine with us, but he seemed to talk with him as much as myself, and by questioning him we obtained a good many points about the surrounding country.

I took a long walk down the creek. The heavy timber entwined with many vines reminded me of the San Antonio Bottoms. The further I went the more I increased my regard for the tall aged trees which, hung with sheets of the ever-present whitish moss, seemed to stand about like so many hoary monuments to time. Their majestic size, their rough and fissured bark, and their twisted and pendant branches, all bore evidence of the many changes of season, the countless storms, and the frequent violent shocks they had known. The air was calm, and but for the hum of thousands of mosquitoes' wings, the swamp was as silent as a tomb. During my long walk I had seen but two or three birds, and these few were very timid, flying at my approach.

Everything in the vicinity shared in the gloom thrown about the deserted village, and, with few exceptions, animal life must have migrated with the people who once occupied the town. We had been eight or ten days at a time without seeing any human being but ourselves, but I had not known a place so sepulchral as this, where even the leaves seemed reluctant to flutter, and as I picked my way through the over-abundant undergrowth, hearing only the tread of my own feet, I thought of myself as trespassing upon some forbidden soil.

Absalom Helped

Emerging from the wood I found Mr. Priour seated upon the ground, busily engaged in repairing the rents Absalom had made in his trousers. We often found it necessary to mend our clothing, and generally employed a darning needle threaded with twine, while for patches we used empty grain sacks or anything else we could find. My own trousers had been patched, patched and quilted until the material of which they were originally made was completely hidden from view, and the stripes which once adorned my partner's nether garments were one by one being buried in rags of other and less brilliant hue.

"Have you been out with your gun?" I asked.

"Yes, I went up the stream a little, but there wa'n't a bird to be seen, and I thought I'd mend my pants where they caught on that nail."

"What nail?" I asked.

"What nail? Why, a nail in that dog-on'd nigger house across here; didn't you hear them tear when I went through the hole that coon butted?"

"No, I thought Absalom tore your pants."

"You thought Absalom tore them? Well, he didn't! How could he tear my pants when he had hold of that kicking coon?"

"I didn't know he touched the fellow, I thought I saw him at your heels all the time."

"Well, you didn't! He wa'n't anywhere about my heels. He was helping his master, and I'd never caught the black hog in a week, if the dog hadn't turned to and bent on with me, which was enough sight more'n you done. What was you doing all that time anyway? You stood as still as you was having pictures taken. Was there anybody around there taking them? Ha! ha! ha!"

"No, I was taking your picture in my mind though, and if I remember right, Absalom wasn't far from your legs all the time. Didn't you turn around three or four times and kick him away from you? If you didn't, what made the dog yell the way he did?"

"He yelled when he caught the nigger's throat, and that yell meant 'I've got him' just as plain to me as though he could talk. He knows niggers as well as I do, and I know them as well as ducks."

"Where is the man now?" I asked.

"Gone back into his hole, I guess. I gave him two minutes to get across the stream and out of sight before I'd sic the dog on him, and if you ever saw a black streak streak off, 'twas him after he saw that dog's eyes and teeth. Absalom was just dying to get another grab at his throttle, and I had to hold him till the cuss'd gone."

Mr. Priour finished his praise of the dog and the mending of his trousers at the same time, and he felt proud of the style in which each had been done.

"I tell you!" he shouted. "There's a patch that's put on to stay and looks a blame sight better than it did before that fool of a dog—that fool of a dogged nail caught in it up there! I'm a patcher!" and he triumphantly waved his breeches aloft before getting into them again.

It was now late and we discussed the question of remaining here over night. Priour thought we had better continue on our way, and not being particularly in love with the gloomy place myself, we packed our wagon and pulled out. I had filled our coffee pot with water from the creek, and carefully stowed it away in the wagon, for we never knew when we were to find more.

In the Dark

A drive of a half-mile through the timber brought us to the edge of the prairie, which spread out before us as far as the eye could reach. There was no worn wagon road here and our only guide was a furrow which had been plowed across the open country from Texana to the Conchoway Creek. This furrow was for the purpose of enabling travelers to keep the right direction in going from one place to the other. There were no wheel marks visible to the casual eye, but by carefully examining the ground we found that one team at least had preceded us since the fall of rain a week before.

The distance to the next creek was much more than our negro captive had stated, and when darkness fell about we were still many miles from the place. The afternoon had been a warm one, and our little stock of water had been drunk three hours before. We were thirsty and eager to reach the stream before halting, and drove on and on, mile after mile, depending upon the horses to follow the furrow, which they had done so nicely while daylight lasted. After a two-hours' drive in the gloom we stopped the team, lighted our lantern, and took a look about us. To our dismay, the horses had lost the trail and we knew not in which direction our course now lay. The animals were tired and as thirsty as ourselves, and I was in favor of camping on the spot until daylight would come to our rescue. It was now near midnight and a rest of three or four hours would have done the team much good. But Priour thought differently.

"Now I'll be dog-on'd if I'm going to be skunked this way," he said. "My hair's too long for me to be cooped up like this."

"What are you going to do?" I asked.

"I'm going to drive on to somewhere; it may be the creek, it may be into a bog, or it may be to Tophet; but I'm going somewhere. This dry sandy prairie ain't any place to spend the night, and I'm going out of it if the horses die to pay for it."

"You may be driving away from the creek all the time."

"Well, it's all the same to me whether we drive up, down, crossways or slanting. I'm going to fetch up somewhere or spend the night in driving. This's all on account of that nigger back at Texana. I knew blame well he couldn't tell the truth about anything. I never saw a nigger yet that could. It's as natural for them to lie as to be black and woolly, I wish he was here now."

"What would you do if he was here?" I asked.

"I'd harness him to this wagon and he'd pull it to the creek inside of ten minutes or he'd die."

Climbing the wagon we started the tired team and moved on again. This time fortune favored us, and after a drive of two or three miles we entered the edge of a copse. This we supposed to be the outskirts of the Conchoway Bottoms, and not knowing whether above or below the road through the wood, we came to camp. Being too thirsty to eat any supper, we spread our tent and blankets under the trees, and went to sleep as soon as possible in order to outwit the sense of thirst.

Three hours later it was growing light, and mounting one of the horses, Mr. Priour started off to search for the road through the timber. During his absence I took a walk among the trees.

Birds were merrily chirping their morning anthems, and the whole forest was alive with praises to the newborn day. These feathered ones were so happy that I refrained from killing any of them; but when I saw a plump little rabbit cutting about among the brush, my heart became a shade harder, and stimulated by the hollow moan from my empty stomach, I took him for my own.

Conchoway Creek

After an absence of two hours or less Mr. Priour returned. He reported that we were about three miles above the road, and that the drive to the creek would be one mile more. He had ridden to the stream, and drank his fill of water "as pure as crystal," and I coveted a portion of it. Absalom, too, had lapped the water, and I felt vexed that he should have quenched his thirst before myself. Harnessing the team once more, and following the edge of the copse for about the distance Priour had stated, we came to the patch cut through the bottoms. This rough and stumpy way led us to Conchoway Creek.

There being so little travel here we thought it perfectly safe to camp in the middle of the road. After leading the horses into the brush where they could browse, we built a fire and cooked the rabbit I had killed a few hours before. The meat was sweet and tender, and Priour pertinently asked why I hadn't shot two of them. After enjoying a bracing smoke we inspected the crossing below us. There was a bridge across the creek, but it was so sadly out of repair that no team could safely go over it. The timbers were rotten, and in places unsupported. This was particularly the case on the far side, where the two outside logs reached only to within a foot or two of the bank beyond, owing to the washing away of the earth rather than the shortening of the sticks. The stream was boggy, and someone had removed the boards from the bridge and placed them in the shallow water by its side, making a sort of flooring over the soft mud. There was abundant evidence that teams had been driven through the stream and over this floor. The soft earth was moulded into figures, grooves and punctures in a style that could have been executed only by horses, wagons and men slumping through the oozy mire.

We had been bogged often enough ourselves to know what signs were gener-ally left where the trial occurred, and the imprint here of naked feet, six inches by fourteen, convinced us that negro ingenuity was responsible for the tearing away of the bridge. The boards could cover only a portion of the muddy way, and were lying promiscuously about in the stream, the water not being deep enough to float them away.

"Well, this is a regular nigger game anyway," said my partner. "Two dollars would have fixed the bridge, but they were too lazy to chop a stick to put in it. I've known a nigger to tear off his ear and bait a trap with it; I've known them to pull down a house to build a hog-pen; but this is the worst I ever did see. I never knew before that they'd rip up a good bridge and ram the boards in the mud like this."

"I suppose we'll have to cross on the boards as they have done," I said.

"I suppose we won't. That mud's deep enough to take our whole business out of sight. Niggers and mud're akin anyway; they'll woller through anything a hog will, but that's no road for a white man to go."

"What are you going to do then?"

"There's only one thing we can do; we'll have to fish out all them boards and cut some logs and mend the bridge. We call do it in a few hours. I don't want to bury my team, and walk to Corpus Christi besides."

We Turn Bridge Engineers

Priour was in earnest, and foregoing all thoughts of a foot-journey through the bottoms, we at once began work. Our hatchet had done service as a cold-chisel, screwdriver, and nail-extractor during our whole tour, and was much the worse for its rough usage; but by often relieving each other in the use of the instrument we managed to fell two six-inch ash trees.

WE TURN BRIDGE ENGINEERS

Shouldering to the bridge the logs thus obtained, we placed them by the sides of the two rotten ones, shoving them far enough upon the bank to have firm support. The two middle timbers running lengthwise were sound and unyielding, and were left undisturbed.

Our next duty was to fish the boards out of the mud. This was dauby business, but we were in a dauby country, and to have shirked the labor would have been decidedly out of order. At first we were a little careful about getting in too deep, but we soon learned that to be too fussy would be to fail in our undertaking, and before the last stick was out we were muddied from head to foot. Placing the reclaimed lumber upon the frame of logs we had made ready for it, we completed our labor, and gazed with pride upon the result of our enterprise.

"There," said my partner. "There's a good job, but the next coons that come along'll pitch the whole thing into the mud again."

"They will?"

"Yes, they will. It's their nature to do just that way. They'd rather swash through mud four feet deep than drive over a dry road any time."

"Do they like mud so well as that?"

"Tain't only mud they're after. They like to yell, and as there's nothing to yell at in crossing a bridge, they'll all pile into the creek and split their dog-on'd throats hollering when they try to shove the wagon through. I suppose they've had more fun in getting bogged in this hole than you can guess."

The Knowing Absalom

It was not yet noon, but our exertions had made us hungry, and taking our guns we went into the brush in search of game. Rabbits were abundant, and had no fear of us, and after taking as many as we could have any use for, I stopped almost within reaching distance of a number of them. These little animals were much better for eating than the jackrabbit. We could always obtain the jacks by dozens, and had tired of them; but these smaller ones tasted so much better that we went out of our way to get them.

Absalom had spent the morning lounging about the wagon, in complete view of us while working on the bridge. The dog was as lank as a ramrod and it seemed rather strange that he had not tried for some of the rabbits feeding all about him. He was glad enough to crunch the bones of the one we had eaten for breakfast, but was too stupid to hunt for them himself.

"Why don't that dog catch some of those rabbits?" I asked of his master.

"Ah-ha!" he replied. "He's not such a traitor as that. He wouldn't leave watching that wagon if he starved to death waiting for us to come back."

"He left our camp at the Cholette, and followed us several miles up the stream, didn't he?"

"Yes, but there wa'n't any niggers about there. He knows when the wagon's safe, and when it ain't."

"We haven't seen any negroes today; how's he to know there are any about here?"

"He knows by the smell, of course. What's his nose for, anyway? He knew as well as I, how that bridge came in the mud."

"How'd he know it?"

"How'd he know it?! Didn't you see him go down and smell of them boards, and then skin back to that wagon with his knowing eyes?"

"No, I didn't see it."

"Well, I knew you didn't; you was gapin' up at that three year-old squirrel nest in that tree when he done it. If you'd keep your wits about you, you wouldn't ask such foolish questions."

"The poor dog, he ought to have something to eat, I should say."

"No, he hadn't—not till we get home, then I'm going to give him a dog-on'd good meal."

CHAPTER IX
IN WHICH WE COLLECT BRIDGE TOLL

We Pose as Inspectors

Our dinner was soon eaten, and seeking the shade of the overspreading branches, we smoked our thanks to the soft bed of leaves upon which we lay. Our enjoyment was supreme, and we might have whiled away the remainder of the day, but for interference.

Immediately back of the far end of the bridge was a slight elevation beyond which the slope was gradual down to the prairie level again. From over this little hill came the sounds: "Hoo-up, dar! Come up! Come up double! Pete! Come up double! Mos' de kreak! Yah, yah, yah! Good golly! He-yeu! Hoo-oo-oo!"

"Some nigger team," said my partner. "Now, I'll see if they tear our work all down and pile it into the creek. If they do, now there'll be a buzzard feast over their carcasses before night."

Keeping ourselves well hidden from sight we watched for the approaching team. It soon mounted the rising ground and came full into our view. Two ragged half-naked negroes, two emaciated horses, and a dilapidated and squeaky wagon formed the assemblage which was making noise enough for a caravan of howling beasts. The men saw our wagon which lay in their path, and they also noticed the changes we had made about the crossing. Halting on the top of the bank they opened their eyes and mouths in amazement.

"Wha dis mean? Who team dat?" one of them asked.

"De bridge 'spectors," returned the other, "dey come aroun here ebery fo' year. Dey in de woods huntin' squirrels now."

"B'squash! Dat too bad. No mo fun in de kreak 'til dey go 'way agin."

"Less go fru de kreak jess same."

"Dey ain' no boads dar now. We neber git fru 'thout boads."

"Less take off some an' put um back 'gin, fo dey come out de woods."

"No, de wagon in de road."

The men had alighted from their wagon, and were walking about, as though strongly tempted to remove some of the boards to the creek. Several times they stepped down the bank as far as the water, and then back again, as though grieved over their blasted expectations.

I likened them to someone who had lost a dear friend, or who had been abroad and returned to find ruins in place of a home, and I was sorry for them. But Mr. Priour had no such feelings and, as the two woebegone men stepped upon the bridge, he emerged from the cover, and with his stentorian voice split the air into divergent gashes like some exploding bomb: "Hey you black dogs! Get off that bridge or I'll fill your hides as full of shot-holes as a sieve."

We Take Toll

This sudden volley of words struck the negroes like a whirlwind and they looked as guilty as though detected in some crime.

"Who ripped this bridge all up by the roots and then scattered boards in that nigger picnic down there?" shouted my partner.

"We doan' know, boss," came the reply. "We dun tryin' fine out who done dat."

"Tell me who did it, or I'll bury you, horses, traps, and all, you hammer-nosed pelts!"

"I—I—I doan' know. T—Tom—Tom Barney, he say de bridge no good. He lif one boad see de punk, and de boad fall in de kreak. De win blow in de kreak, too."

"What'd you say about taking these boards off and sliding in the mud again, before we came out of the woods?"

"No, sah! We come up here fix de bridge. Boads in de bosh no good, Mr. 'Spector. We on yo side."

"Well, you're on the other side of the creek anyway and you'll have to pay toll to get across. We ain't going to work here a week for nothing. Give me four bits and I'll let your traveling hog-yard over."

"Good golly!" exclaimed the negro. "Dat's more 'n I seed for a year, Mr. 'Spector. I send de money in a letter nex week."

"No, you won't. What've you got under them dirty rags in the wagon?"

"Aigs."

"Where are you going with eggs?"

"Victori."

"Victori," sneered Priour, "you won't get there with that horse in a month."

"O yes, we git dar free days mo, sho."

"Well, give me twenty eggs and I'll let you over, and mind they're good ones, too; I've eat too many rotten eggs to be fooled on them more'n twenty deep."

"Yes sah, I gib yer good aigs: de rotten ones down de bottom ter sell ignorancy folks."

"Well, give us the top ones then."

At first I thought Priour was joking, but he insisted upon having the toll, which the negro gladly gave from his many dozen. Eggs were cheap and the blacks' wagon was full of them, but how they had expected to get through the boggy stream without spilling the entire load, could have been explained only by African science.

Carefully stowing away our dishonest eggs, we harnessed our team and drove over the bridge. The boards were loose and the logs upon which they lay round; but both were quite firm and would have stood much more strain than we taxed them with. As might have been expected, the negroes asked for tobacco, and after I had furnished each with a chew, they bade us a good day and went over the bridge in the direction we had come.

From what Priour had told me and from what I had heard myself during the blacks' conversation, I thought it quite probable that the men might halt in the timber, wait until we were out of sight, and then return to demolish the bridge and souse the "traveling hog-yard" through the bog. Their wagon bore every sign of practical acquaintance with the bog-sliding art, and another coat of Concho-way sizing would have stiffened up the spokes, axles and tires.

Our own road lay over the prairie again, and we wished to reach the next stream twenty miles away, before night.

Absalom is Fastened

Mr. Priour feared Absalom would stray from us and follow the negroes to Victoria. The dog constantly lagged behind, and although several times coaxed to us, he dropped back again just as soon as the team was started. This disconcerted the man and he asked me: "Do you know what's the matter with that dog?"

"I suppose he wants to go back and see that those negroes don't tear our work all down again, doesn't he?" I asked.

"No he don't; now we're over, he don't care more'n I do what becomes of the bridge."

"What is the matter with him then?"

"Well, I'll tell what the matter is. Them coons give him a love powder!"

"What's that?" I asked.

"Don't you know what a love powder is? Why it's something the blame cusses get in the swamp. Don't ever take anything from a nigger; now I warn you."

"What'll a love powder do? How do they give them, and what do they taste like?"

"They give them in anything they can find, and if they'd got you to take one, you'd been hanging back like Absalom, and I'd had to go back and—no, I'll be blowed if I would. I'd let you go on with them and marry a yellar gal till you come out of the spell. How'd you like to have fifteen or twenty woolly-headed children to take back home with you?"

"I don't think I would care for as many as that."

"No sir, I wouldn't touch anything a black man's hand ever saw, if I knew it."

"How do you know but there are some love powders in the eggs? Perhaps they hope to bring back a whole string of white people from Victoria."

"I don't know; but I can tell by the smell."

"You'll have to kill Absalom if he don't follow us, won't you?"

"No I won't, I'll tie him to the wheel and he'll follow, I reckon."

Priour had no intention of losing his pet, and searched the wagon for something with which to bind him. The sole piece of line available for such a purpose was less than two feet in length, and the only practicable way to use it effectively, was to place the dog's head upon the upper side of the rear axle, and lash it firmly in place. This was soon done, and although the lovesick one's fore feet were lifted clear of the ground, his master thought he could get along on the other two, after a fashion.

The trouble with Absalom had delayed us not a little, and after making him secure, we mounted our seat, and urged the horses onward. Shortly after the sun had set, we sighted a line of timber several miles distant, and at dark crossed the stream hidden therein, and camped in a clearing just beyond. We had paid no attention to Absalom during the long drive; Priour had forgotten all about him, and I didn't care much whether he left us for other company or not. But when we came to free him, our nerves were shocked. Poor dog; his head had remained on the axle as we had bound it, and in driving rapidly over the rough unbroken ground, the wagon had pounded upon the top of his skull and flattened it out like a serpent's. There was plenty of room for two heads when we had fastened the one there, but we were on the ground then, and as the seat was in the middle of the wagon, our weight must have closed up the space fully one-half.

In spite of this mutilation, the dog clung to life, or life to him, but his limbs were weak and he could lie down much easier than he could walk. He must have been dragged the last few miles, if not the most of the long drive, and I was glad that it was Absalom and not myself that was under the love powder spell.

"Now I'll be dog-on'd," said Priour, "that's too mean a trick to play on any man; he's too sick to stand up and I'd forgot all about him. Didn't you think of him?"

"Yes, I thought of him, but he has a tongue and a throat; why didn't he whine when he was being hurt?"

"Now he ain't the whining kind; he'd stay where his master put him if he died a thousand deaths!"

"You'll have to kill him now, won't you?" I asked.

"No I won't, I'm going to give him a good supper, if I go 'thout myself and you too. We've got rabbits and eggs enough to pay for all of this."

Priour was really grieved at the new shape of the dog's head, and he endeavored to press it back into its original form by squeezing it between his hands. This was somewhat painful to the patient, and he made so much complaint that the operation had to be abandoned.

We soon had a pleasant campfire, and taking coffee pot in hand, I went to the creek for water, while my partner made preparations to make a pie of our eggs and rabbit. The evening was rather dark, and I had some difficulty in getting the pot full of clear water. I could get it half-full without I trouble; but to find a place deep enough to sink the vessel, necessitated some prospecting. By experience I knew how treacherous the earth commonly was about Texan streams, and being wholly unacquainted in the place, I moved with great caution, poking my way about with a stick.

Mr. Priour in a New Role

I had been absent from camp nearly a half hour before finding a good watering place that was approachable, and fearing my partner might give everything to Absalom before my return, I hurried back toward camp again. When I had mounted the little rise of ground near the stream, the bright campfire came within my range of sight, and everything in its near presence could be distinctly seen. Mr. Priour was engaged in a work I had never known him to do before— he was scouring out our stew-pan with earth, and if his salvation had depended upon his doing the work quickly and well, he could not have shown more vigor in the task. The ground all about was covered with sward, but it was an easy matter to open it with a heroic boot heel, and with his hands alone the man was shoveling and scrubbing in a manner that told me something had happened.

Moving a little nearer to the scene, my nose discovered to me the probable cause of the untiring energy of my companion—rotten eggs! I not only smelled, but breathed and tasted them. It seemed hardly possible that twenty eggs could have bred such an odor, and I was nauseated. The usual way of preparing eggs in Texas is to fill a stew-pot with them and mash with the foot, picking the shells out after the dish is cooked. This is to get the seasoning of the shell and foreign matter therefrom, and as Priour had followed this rule, every egg had been broken. Neither of us was much afraid of eating from a pot a little soiled, and as this was the first time there had been any attempt at cleaning culinary utensils since our leaving Corpus Christi, I believe there was more cause for it than a score of stale eggs.

"What's the matter?" I asked as I entered the circle of light.

"Matter enough!" shouted Priour. "Here's a fine mess; what do you suppose I found in them nigger eggs?"

"I should think by the smell, you had found rotten eggs in them."

"Well I didn't, they were as sound as when laid; but the last dog-on'd one of them had a love powder in it. Whew! Don't you smell them?"

"I smell rotten eggs. Those negroes deceived us and we are sold. Their privilege of crossing the bridge didn't cost them an egg."

"Yes it did; it cost them twenty of them. Look here; do you suppose I'd scrape the skin all off my hands just for a poor egg! I guess I wouldn't, but I wouldn't touch a love powder for anything. I guess the pot's clean enough now to cook a rabbit; we'll have to risk it anyway."

Mr. Priour's contention had been to convince me that he was afraid of love powders, but he failed to do so. He was not a cautious man, and in scrubbing our only cooking utensil he had some other object in view than ridding it of Voodoo influence. Probably he had hoped to conceal all traces of the spoiled eggs before my return, and to account for the disappearance in some plausible way. He didn't like the idea of being beaten by negroes, and I am sure could have disposed of the egg question satisfactorily to himself had I remained at the creek a few minutes longer. This conclusion of mine became more certain upon my discovering a place where the man had tried to bury the broken eggs, and had failed to cover them completely, only on account of the darkness.

By frying meat until tender, before boiling it, we often made a stew in the fractional part of an hour, and on this occasion our meal was soon ready to be served.

Absalom's Lost Opportunity

True to his word, my partner presented a choice portion to Absalom. But alas! The first time for weeks that the animal had been offered food, he was unable to eat. He nosed the savory mixture a little and tried to partake, but his mouth and throat were in no condition to do so, and with an expression of defeated hope, he turned away and sought the shelter of the wagon. Here he kept as quiet as an image, and had he been a valuable dog, I should have prophesied a death in the camp before morning.

It was well for us that the maimed animal could not use his jaws, for the stew was a good one, and after our own stomachs were filled, there was little left but naked bones.

CHAPTER X
LOOKING FOR STRAYED HORSES

At daybreak we were on our feet again, and visiting the patient under the wagon, we saw that he had greatly improved during the night. He could walk fairly well and could even chew a little on the bones we had left from supper.

"This all comes from good care," said Priour. "He'd a been dead in less than an hour if I hadn't given him that medicine."

"What medicine?" I asked, "And what care did he have?"

"What care did he have! Didn't you see me go into the woods and get them herbs and steep for his head?"

"No, I didn't see you. Where was I when you did all that?"

"You was snoozing like a hog. Why, I was bathing Absalom's head half the night with the best medicine that grows."

"What kind of herbs did you get for the dog?"

"Hammer-skull root and hidepatch; they'll cure any kind of hammering or peeling about the head. I reckon Absalom's all right." And the man avoided further questioning by taking his gun and leaving camp.

I Shoot a Heron

Picking up my gun, I also went forth to explore the bottoms and search for birds. Following the edge of the watercourse I went far up the bottoms. I found Mississippi kites in goodly numbers. They were the first we had seen since leaving Corpus Christi, and I killed several of them. But aside from the satisfaction of a stroll among the endless variety of nature's expressions, my trip was an unremunerative one, and I was glad to be at camp again. Mr. Priour had met with no more success in hunting than I, and we voted the place a dry one for birds.

After lounging about the wagon a while, I became thirsty, and with the ever-ready coffee pot went for some water. When I had reached the creek, I saw on its farther side, standing upon a piece of driftwood, a fine snowy heron. To see one of these beautiful birds is to want it, and slipping back to camp I seized my gun, returned and shot it. As it was on the other side of the stream from me, and under the steep bank, I was at a loss to know how to get at my prize. I could find no pole long enough to reach it. I couldn't well get across the water myself, and had I stood on the other side, the bird would have been out of reach below me. Mr. Priour came to my relief and tried to lasso the fowl, but the latter was too near the vertical bank for the line to go over him, and another scheme was proposed and carried out by my partner.

Near where we were standing was a drift log, long enough to reach across to the other side, but there was nothing upon which the end might rest, and I could see no way in which the stick could be made useful to us. My partner saw a way, however, and while standing in mud knee-deep, with a kind of battering ram motion he pounded one end of the log about six inches into the soft bank opposite us.

This done, the man struck the attitude of a tight-rope walker for an instant, and then started across the oozy chasm. I admired his courage, for I knew how unpleasant it was to have dealings with an unexpected mud bath, and as much as I desired the heron, I would not have attempted such a feat as this to get it.

Mr. Priour walked safely over the muddy mixture, and stooping, was about to seize the bird, when, in order to balance himself a little more accurately, it became necessary to make a violent gesture; this quick movement surprised the log and sent its end free and clear from the slippery socket. Slipping from his uncertain perch, the man vanished completely from view in the sand and water. An instant later his head appeared, and ejecting a muddy stream from both mouth and nostrils, he wallowed ashore with the well-earned trophy.

It was too shady under the trees for anything to dry, and going out on the end of the prairie, Mr. Priour spread himself and the heron to the sun. Here the man fell asleep, and the buzzards came and ate the muddy bird.

The day was a warm one, and in two hours my partner's clothes were dry enough to suit him. He liked them a little damp, he said, for they were softer, and the late incident had not only made his raiment more pliable, but had been the means of his enjoying a good long nap. After such mishaps as the one he had just known, Priour was ordinarily an optimist.

A Queer Place for Horses

We had, this morning, left our horses in the brush a short distance from camp, and not until all else was ready for the start, did we learn that they had strayed. We struck into the woods, to hunt for the missing team, Priour taking a course up the stream, while I went in the opposite direction. I soon forgot all about my mission, and spent the time in admiring nature. In hundreds of places the earth was deeply cut by chasms too wide to leap across, and too long to go around. Often, the walls of these cuts were not too steep to climb, and as I worked my way through and among them, I likened myself to a mouse climbing over a field of ditches. Two hours after leaving camp, I was still prospecting the mazy fissures, but had traveled little distance in a direct line.

At the bottom of one of these gulches I saw an opening which I thought might lead to the home of some burrowing owl or animal, and wishing to learn all about the matter, I climbed the bank, cut a long stick and returned to examine the cavity. The tunnel-like passage was a long one, and being zealous in my undertaking, I did not hear approaching footsteps above, and had no knowledge that I was being watched, until I heard the words: "Now I'll be dog-on'd if that ain't a queer place to hunt for a horse. Do you suppose you could get them out with that stick if they were in there?"

Priour had taken me by surprise, but I quickly recovered myself and replied: "I don't see any other place about here where they could stow away."

"Well, you can throw away your ramrod and come back to camp," he returned. "I found them horses and had them harnessed before you'd been gone ten minutes, and we're behind two hours."

"Why didn't you discharge your gun?" I asked.

"Why didn't I discharge my gun?! Well, do you come to me every time I shoot a bird, and haven't I fired a dozen times for you in the last hour? You must be deaf or stupid, and if I hadn't found you in ten minutes, I was going on alone, and you'd had to got a rabbit out of that hole, or gone without your supper."

"You wouldn't leave me like that, would you?"

"Yes, I would. Next time we hunt the team, soon's I find them, you come back."

"Suppose I should find them and leave you?" I asked.

"Well, you've never found them yet when they were lost, and I'll risk it."

Priour was correct in his statement that I had never found the team. I always found some occupation that I preferred to hunting stray horses, and as it is customary in Texas for a person to do just as he pleases until killed for it, I shirked all team-hunting duty and freely admitted my uselessness in this line.

Absalom Restrains Himself

It was nearly sunset when we left the bottoms for the prairie. Absalom was able to travel by the side of the wagon and manifested no desire to leave us. If the pounding on his head hadn't driven the love powder out, it had at least given fit punishment for his foolishness and taught him a lesson.

The level ground was covered with masses of coarse knotted grass, and the number of skunks to be seen running about was unpleasantly suggestive of what might happen to us before morning, for we were to spend the night somewhere on the prairie. Absalom would be no protection to us. His experience at the live oaks had satisfied him that the most discreet course would be to have no business with such animals. He trotted by the side of the wagon as though unconscious of the scores of them running about within a few yards of him. I had never before seen these fetid creatures so thick. They were of various colors, white, black and brown. I believe that we could have counted a hundred during our two-hour drive.

I was disgusted with our dog; he wouldn't even sniff at the enemies, and I said to Priour: "What's the matter with Absalom? Why don't he sail in and clean out these pests?"

"Ah ha!" he laughed. "That dog's no such fool as that; he's saving his wind till night, when he'll need it to guard our camp. I tell you that dog's got a long head!"

"That all may be true," I replied, "but I'd like to see him tackle one of them, just to see what he can do."

"Well, he won't do it, he knows better. Why, he's got all he can do now to keep his wrath down; don't you see how he carries his head. He's afraid he can't hold in much longer, and knows if he gets a kill in on one of them, he can't stop till he drops."

"Suppose I 'sic' him on one of them?"

"Don't you do it; you might just as well fire away all your ammunition to see if 'twas good, and then be without any. I tell you that animal's nobody's fool!"

Driving until it was quite dark, we hauled our wagon just out of the path, and spread our bedding upon the tall grass which was now thoroughly wet by the heavy dew. So great was my fear of a visit from skunks, that I proposed spending the night on our unevenly loaded wagon. I had no confidence in Absalom, and did not wish to repeat my encounter with one of the nocturnal callers while in the live oaks. But my partner persuaded me to sleep upon the ground, and I reluctantly deferred to his opinion that we would not be molested while so near a dog, whether the latter was living or dead.

At such times as this, Priour's unconcern was enviable. No matter what threatened, he could lie down and go to sleep at any time or in any place, as much at ease as if in his own bedchamber. This was fortunate for him, for if he had fretted as much as I about what might happen, he would have pined and been blown away by some north wind, years before. His sleep, though, was rarely disturbed, and whether this was a case of "from cause to effect," or "effect to cause," or simply a coincidence, I could not decide; but the fact remained that I was always on the lookout for pestiferous company, and generally found it.

A Texas Signboard

On this evening I borrowed more trouble than I had use for, for our sleep was undisturbed until early dawn, when the horses awoke us. We usually tied but one of these animals up at night, as they were company for each other, and securing one was sufficient. The one so secured was generally Gruya, while Whitie was allowed full liberty, and to keep our sack of grain from the latter's reach Priour used it as a pillow. Whitie knew what the grain sack was and where it could be found, and he was in the habit of slipping up to our bed during the night, seizing this bag between his teeth and dragging it from under the sleeping man. The sudden dropping of his head so caused, often awoke my partner, and although he would replace the grain and whip the horse besides, the latter would try the same thing again whenever he was hungry.

Once in a while the fall would not awaken the man, and Whitie would shake the sack until its contents were spilled, and then crunch corn to his satiation. This would arouse envious feelings in Gruya, who, being tethered, could only enjoy the sound of the process of grinding, and his nervous pawing of the ground when thus tantalized, had frequently been the cause of our waking and rescuing the food. On this morning we were brought to our senses in such a manner.

It had been a clear starry night, and our upper blanket and the herbage about us were as wet with dew as if rained upon. Our couch was dry, and it seemed like jumping overboard, to get out into the grass.

An hour's drive brought us to a fork in the road, near which was a large guide-board, wired to a post. This board bore hieroglyphic letters, which must have been put on with a chewed stick, years before:

RIGHT HAND TO BUNDICK'S FERRY
PARAMOUNT ROAD. NO BOGS.
ALL OTHER FERRY-BOATS BOG ALL OVER.
COME ON. ONLY 3 MILES.

Having no wish to patronize a ferryboat that was bog all over, and seeing that the right trail had been used much more than the left, we took the former, and an hour later were at the bottoms of the Colorado river.

Priour Assumes Dignity

Driving through this timber we reached the stream. Near this was a clearing and the ferryman's home—a comfortable looking dwelling, but from the many large boggy depressions in the ground about it, it must have been unpleasantly wet in a rainy season. The ferryman was away on an alligator hunt, but a six-mile neighbor left in his place, was glad to see us, and like everyone else we met, he was anxious to know our business with such a load of boxes, bales and bags.

"Are you boring for oil?" he asked.

"No," returned Priour. "We're surveying and are going to draw a map of the State for the Governor."

"What's the Guvner want a map for?"

"He wants to know where this dog-on'd river sprouts from, and we're going to find out too, if we're hung for it."

"Well, now here; I heard tell of a feller that sold charts to a school house. Can you tell if there's any difference from charts and maps?"

"Yes, I can tell you," replied the recently endowed scientist. "There's no heft of difference, only a chart is signed by the people who live on it, and a map by the Governor."

"Are these maps of yourn for sale?"

"Yes."

"Well, I want one to hang up in my house. I allus did like I to study maps. How much are they?"

"Five dollars apiece."

"Well, I don't know's I care for one today. My boy ain't growed up yet and can't read it—he's who I wanted it for. When you come this way again, stop and I'll buy one."

In the nearly dry ponds about this spot there were many pretty freshwater shells, and at the expense of getting in the mud up to my knees I fished out a few of them. This performance was also a singular thing to the inquisitive man, who asked what the shells were to be used for; Priour appositely answered: "To figger on."

"Well, I never heard of that before," came the reply, "and here I've been reckoning dedit and loss in the mud with a stick for years. I wished you fellers'd come around here before. Can't you draw a map on one of them shells for me now?"

"No," returned my partner. "We've got to make calculations of devaporation from away off here and reckon up from it. We've got to work up from the bottom and couldn't draw a map now any more'n you could measure a peck of corn when you hadn't got but a handful of it."

"Well, I'll be goshed! I never heard such edjecation before. Look here, ain't you the Guvner himself with his other clothes on?"

"Ah-ha!" laughed Priour. "I guess that's most too personal a question just now." Assuming the dignity of a four-story chief magistrate he sternly commanded: "Get that hog trough of a boat ready for us as quick as you know how to move!"

The ferryman obsequiously obeyed this fierce charge, and we were soon on the other side of the narrow stream. Here the stranger received his four bits, bowed with extreme courtesy and returned with his craft.

Always Take Your Hat Off

The water was deep, and the bank soft and spongy, but we reached hard footing without accident. There was no house on this side of the river, and as the ferryman's home across was some distance from the bank, a person wishing to cross from the side we were now on, must have some way of making his wants known. The cunning Texan had provided means for such communication, and on a tree by the river there hung a large rusty tin pan, and over this a notice which read:

WHEN YOU WANT TO COME OVER THE RIVER
HAMMER ON THIS PAN WITH A CLUB,
BING, BANG, BUNG

This Texan gong bore every evidence of severe usage, and could not have been depended upon for carrying fine water. Mr. Priour could not pass unheeded such an invitation as was extended by the notice, and seizing a heavy cudgel with both hands he began to hammer away—Bing, Bang, Bung. He showered the blows thick and fast, only stopping when the object of his attack lay scattered about the tree upon which it had hung; then dropping his club he said: "There, I've done's the sign told me to, and I reckon I've done it good enough, too."

"What did you do that for?" I asked.

"What'd I do it for?! Don't it say on that sign to hammer the pan *Bang, Bung, Bog, Bangy, Bungy, Bug*."

"Yes, but that isn't all it says."

"What else does it say? I didn't see anything but that."

"Don't you see what there is at the top of the notice?"

"O, dog-on, the top. I ain't got up there yet. I begun at the bottom and read it up. What's it say do next, beat the shingle off the tree?" With another blow with the recovered club, he beat the rude notice into splinters.

"What'll the ferryman say when he finds out what you've done?" I asked.

"He'll say I've done my duty like a good Governor. I tell you, I found out long ago that when you're in Rome, you must do like Romans. Now, when I lived at the Papalote, we boys got up a big funeral one time, and put up a sign for everybody to take his hat off. There was one fellow though that ambled right up with his head sheet on, and the first thing he knew he was scraping the bark all off the trunk of a tree that he landed on. Now, I tell you, you'd better read all signs and mind them; it'll save you trouble sometime, perhaps."

Driving a short distance we camped at the foot of a large knoll, and by the side of a lake. Here we pitched our tent, for we expected to stay about the place for several days.

CHAPTER XI
ABSALOM AND THE JABSNAKE

I Experiment

The lake near which we camped, like all wet places in the vicinity, was boggy beyond description. Below this there were several other lakes, but mostly dry. One was so dry that by moving quickly I could walk across its fluctuating bottom.

Birds were abundant about the lake, but as they almost invariably fell into the mud when shot, it was difficult to get them. The mud was bottomless, and to secure any specimen falling therein, we had to drag logs and driftwood down from under the trees and build a walk out to it. This was greasy business, for the logs were as slippery as a piece of New England soap, and each prize secured was the occasion of one or more falls into the mire.

Prothonotary warblers had collected in great numbers at these lakes, and we secured several dozen fine specimens of this desirable bird. Herons of various species were also common. Toward night I wounded a white heron. This bird has a neck something less than a fathom in length, and although I heard much of their pugnacity and the force of their sharp beak backed by the elasticity of a long main-spring, I had classed such information with much other of a like nature concerning various animals and things in Texas, and which I knew to be false. Thus I fearlessly approached my prize. Seizing it by the legs I raised it from the ground, when, like a flash of lightning, the closed and pointed beak swept through the air and struck me fair in the temple. For an instant I thought I had been shot, and quickly dropped my assailant and myself, too.

The blood flowed freely from the wound in my head and I was somewhat dazed. The bird eyed me and I reciprocated its eying. After cleaning my stab as best I could with leaves, I picked up my prisoner again; this time, however, I grasped its neck firmly in order to prevent another thrust. I was thus convinced that at least one yarn spun by the Texan hunters I had met was founded on fact, but wishing to satisfy myself beyond any reasonable doubt, I refrained from killing the bird at once, thinking the practical information I hoped to get would justify the means adopted.

Priour and Absalom were at camp when I returned, and carefully laying my bird on the ground near the dog, I waited for developments. I was not kept waiting long. Absalom had a weakness for nosing game, and soon had his face in a position favorable for an assault. Before long the dagger-like bill shot an inch into the cur's hide as though fired from a gun, and with a howl of pain the animal dashed off to hide himself in the brush.

"What's the matter with that dog?" shouted Priour, who had been busily engaged in skinning a bird at the time.

"I don't know; I guess he must have stepped on a brier or something."

"No, he didn't step on a brier or something! You kicked him in the ribs or else he's bit by a rattlesnake or stung by a jabsnake. He's no dog to act that way about a brier. What'd you kick him for?"

"I didn't kick him."

"Did you see any snake?"

"No, not exactly, but I thought I caught a glimpse of something shooting out toward him."

"That was a jabsnake! They dart out of their holes and jab anything in their reach."

"What do they jab with?" I asked.

"They jab with a jabber; they have a horn on their nose like a swordfish, and it's as poison as greaser soup. We must hunt up that dog and doctor him," and leaving his bird half-skinned, he started off to search for his wounded pet.

It was now getting late in the day, and by the time I had skinned and stuffed my heron, darkness was approaching. By the time the coffee for supper had become hot, the man had returned with his dog. Absalom didn't appear much the worse for the stab he had received, but I noticed that he made a large circle around the stuffed heron which lay on the ground near where his master had passed.

"Now, I'll tell you what," said Priour, "that dog's a keen one. He just knows as much as a doctor. What do you suppose he was doing when I found him?"

"Perhaps he was putting a poultice on his wound," I answered.

"Well, that's pretty near what he *was* doing. There ain't anything in this world any better for a jabsnake's jab than dirt, and he was curled up under some brush just as near the ground as he could get."

"Is he much hurt?" I asked.

"Is he much hurt?! Well, if you had a hole punched in your hide big enough to put your finger in, would you call it hurt? Yes, he's hurt right bad, and we'll have to favor him some for a day or two, I guess."

"Are you going to give him any supper?"

"No, sir. No supper tonight. That'd be bad for his poison, but we won't let him hunt quite so much tomorrow, I guess."

The remark that the dog would not be allowed to hunt so much was music to my ears. His hunting maneuvers had always turned out to be more advantageous to the game than to the huntsmen, and I pictured myself on the morrow, creeping upon birds as carefully as I wished, with the many-tongued traitor lashed to the wagon wheel, unable to dash on and sound an alarm.

CHAPTER XII
IN WHICH WE FIND OUR HORSES

After breakfast the next morning our first duty was to hunt for the horses which had broken their lines and strayed away. Prior went upstream and I down. I took my time and traveled leisurely. I was a bird hunter and anxious to remain at the lakes another day, while my partner was bent on leaving the place at once, and as usual, I left the horse-hunting for him. After tramping a mile or more down the stream, I rounded the lower end of one of the lakes and returned by the bank of the Colorado. The strip of land between these two bodies of water was heavily wooded by large trees closely grown, and the walk was an enjoyable one. With the exception of herons, birds did not here appear in large numbers, probably on account of the scarcity of undergrowth.

I expected Mr. Priour would have found the horses and been in waiting for me upon my return, but upon reaching camp I was somewhat surprised to find a strange man seated upon one of our logs, and as much at home as if monarch of all he could behold. This person had the appearance of a professional vagabond. His clothes were in tatters and his unshaven face bore not the expression of an honest man.

I Am Not Hospitable

"Been huntin' yer hosses, stranger?" were the words that greeted me.

"Yes," I replied. "They have strayed somewhere, probably up the river, and my partner will likely find them."

"Yes, hosses will lose," he said, "but my opinion is they ain't upstream, no-how."

"Where do you suppose they are?" I asked; "I've been a mile or more downstream and haven't seen them."

"O, I don't know where they be, but if ye could make it a object ter me, perhaps I might help ye hunt um up."

"I guess my partner will find them," I returned, "for he is a good horse hunter."

"Now what'll ye bet yer pard'll find um? I wuz brought up right in this country. I know hosses from A ter Z, and yer pard don't know a hoss from a nigger. If ye'll give me a dollar I'll find um for ye afore he gits back."

I informed the visitor that I should do nothing of the sort without first consulting my comrade, whereupon he laughed and said: "Well, if ye want yer hosses gim me a dollar, but if yer wait till yer pard gits back I'll charge ye two. Gimme a dollar an' I'll be off."

This demand I peremptorily refused to comply with, and I was somewhat anxious for the return of Mr. Priour. I didn't like the looks of my caller at all, but as he seemed so anxious to get some money out of me before the return of my companion, it was evident that he wished to avoid seeing that man. Upon my refusal to employ him the stranger haughtily strode away from camp and I breathed easier as the distance between us increased. But he did not go far. He soon returned, and, halting a few yards from me said: "What kind of a gun have ye? Let me see it. I'm some of a gunner myself an' like ter handle um."

This request was an unexpected one and I knew not just how to meet it. The man had thus far shown no signs of hostility and it was a simple thing to ask of me. I had often shown my gun to strangers, and if I had been called upon for a reason for refusing, I could not have given one. But nevertheless I had a feeling about me that I didn't want my gun in that man's hands, and I distinctly told him that I preferred to keep the instrument in my own possession.

"O well," he replied, "if yer afraid I'll hurt it ye can keep it. 'Twon't be anything new fer me ter hold one anyway."

We Find the Steeds

Just as the man finished his remarks Mr. Priour came in sight. I was glad of this, for I thought if there was anything wrong about the visitor, my partner would soon find it out. When the latter had come within talking distance I said to him: "Here's a man that wants to hunt our horses for us; he says he can find them very easily."

"Well, if he can find them so very easy he's a thief and has stole them," and addressing his words to the stranger he said: "Do you know where them horses are?"

"No," came the reply, "but perhaps I could find um for ye if ye'd gimme a couple bits fer terbacker."

"Two bits!" shouted Priour, "I'll give you two bits! I'll give you two charges of No. 4 shot if you don't fetch them horses out in five minutes."

"I ain't got yer hosses."

"No, but you've drove them off and hid them, and I'll blow the top of your head off if you don't show me where they are!"

Mr. Priour was angry to his boots, and cocking his gun he leveled it at the thieving vagabond. The latter, finding the kind of man he had to deal with, became very docile, and followed by my partner, gun in hand, he left the camp for the lost animals.

Picking up my gun, I too followed, and after leading us a quarter mile at right angles to the river, our unwilling guide turned to the right and soon entered a gulch densely grown with tall trees. Here, where they had evidently been driven, we found our two missing horses.

"There, now you git!" shouted Priour, "or I'll give you something to remember me by; I'm no man to have horses stole and then hire the thief to drive them back again!"With the expression of a whipped dog our guide then went his own way, and mounting the horses, Priour and I rode back to camp.

Telling my partner of how the man had asked for my gun and been refused it he said: "Well, if you'd given him that gun you'd never seen it again afterwards. When he found he couldn't get a dollar out of you he thought he'd try for your gun. He's a thief right on his face. I'm almost sorry I didn't kill him anyway."

"He was about camp when I came up from below. Why didn't he go through our tent and steal something?" I asked.

"He might not've got there till just as you did, and there ain't anything in the camp worth stealing anyway. He'd sooner had a dollar for buying gin than to stole all the birds we've got. If Absalom'd only been well, he'd have skinned him alive. He knows such cusses as that as far as he can smell them."

"Yes, I wished Absalom was with me when I was talking about my gun. The dog was at camp when we left here. Did he come up the stream to meet you?"

"Well, now, if you'd been stung by a snake, would you turn out to hunt horses or to drive a man from camp? I tell you that dog's sick enough to die, only he don't want to leave us."

Absalom had lain under the tree a few yards from camp during the whole time of the visit, as if unconscious of anything unusual, but his master was ready with an excuse for him, as he had been many times before. It seemed as though it would have been impossible for the dog to do anything to displease his master, and with the exception of Absalom's friendship with the pigs at the Cholette Creek, Priour had humored the animal in all of his eccentricities.

CHAPTER XIII
TALK AND COFFEE

When about two miles from the bottoms, we saw by the trail far ahead of us, what we took to be the home of some Texan family.

Houses were extremely unusual on our journey, and we hurried the horses on, hoping to have a chat with the people about the place. As we approached the cabin we saw a man come out to the edge of the road and stand as if waiting for our arrival, and he was soon joined by a woman, who we decided was his wife. Drawing nearer, we could see that their faces became wreathed with smiles. They welcomed us as though their dearest friends. I had never received so hearty a welcome from strangers before, and for a moment I could only think that they had taken us for some expected friends, with whom they were unacquainted. They talked with us very pleasantly, asking many questions of our business, travels, etc. They had known of our whereabouts during the last two days, and clearly had been anticipating a chance to talk with us. There was but little travel on the road, and it must have been as much of a treat to these people to see a new face and hear a new voice as it was for us. Perhaps is was more so, for although we were much pleased, they seemed in ecstasy, like children with some new playmate. The man was a typical specimen of a large-hearted Texan—rough and somewhat uncouth in his manners, but generous, and in his way interesting.

Of course they invited us to take a cup of coffee with them—such being the conventional way here of sealing friendship for the time at least—a cup of coffee all around being to the Texan what the pipe of peace is to the Indian. The house occupied by these people was a very rickety affair, and I hesitated to enter lest it should fall and bury us in its ruins. But the man assured me it was perfectly safe, and even should it tumble, he said, no harm could befall us, as the material of its construction was very light, being principally of barrel staves. I had often wondered why so many houses in the State were built of staves, and this man's remark threw much light on the subject. Their house had often blown down, and I might have known that, in falling, heavy timbers would be likely to injure someone. There are many houses in Corpus Christi and for miles about it, built entirely of such material, and to a person awaking in the night by the collapsing of his house, it must be a consoling thought that he is in no danger of being hurt. At any rate, these people spoke with pride of their safety in case of a high wind.

The furniture within this house was most simple. A table, a bed, and four or five rough stools, all homemade and of the same material as the building, were about all of their possessions which we could see, and as the house contained but one room, we probably saw all. They had a few cooking utensils, but the actual cost of everything visible could not have been more than five dollars. Still, they appeared happy, and perhaps enjoyed life as much as if worth many thousands.

Coffee That Is Coffee

We drank of their decoction called coffee, but I failed to perceive any taste that would suggest there being anything in it but old rags and tarred rope. Its flavor sickened me, but I thought it my duty to drink anyway. Mr. Priour drank his as though it was the real article and of his own making. The man and his wife, too, seemed to sip it with pleasure.

I was greatly concerned as to the kind of coffee used, and the method of preparing it, but I hesitated to ask any questions for fear of wounding the feelings of the happy couple. But they both seemed so jolly and laughed so heartily that I soon overcame my feeling of reserve and said: "I have drunk a good many kinds of coffee, but this is of a new flavor to me. Do you mind telling how you make it?"

"Ha! ha! ha! ha!" laughed the man. "Now you've asked it. Ha! ha! ha! You've asked the question. Ha! ha! ha! Haw! haw! You've asked the question that everybody asks. I tell you, sir, my wife made this coffee. My wife makes coffee she does, and when she makes coffee she makes *coffee*!! No soupy slops from her, but k-o-r-f-fy!" and he brought his fist down upon the table with a blow that shook every barrel stave in the shanty.

I had by this time drank nearly all of the mixture which had been given me, and was congratulating myself upon my success in doing what at first seemed impossible. But I was not to be let off so easily.

A Feminine Accomplishment

"Drink to the health of the woman who makes the best coffee in the land," said our host, filling again to the brim my pint up; and, becoming more and more eloquent at every sound from his own lips, he continued: "Drink! drink! drink! And tell everyone you see, where the woman lives that makes good coffee. Why, my dear man," with a blow upon my shoulder that nearly dislocated the bone, "everybody asks about our coffee. How to make it can't be told; 'tis years of experience that's taught the secret."

"Perhaps he doesn't like the coffee," said the hostess, whose face had been all aglow at her husband's eulogy upon her skill.

"Like it!" said I. "It is rich! It is nectar! It tastes of honeysuckles and roses. Great Scott! What stuff it would be to bait hummingbird traps with! Hurrah for the coffee maker!" And rising to my feet I drained my cup as I would have done had it contained a potion of castor oil. I then made a dash for the open air, and reached the vicinity of our wagon before my stomach revolted against such a mixture, which it soon did. Being relieved of the full quart of prairie coffee I felt better, and was soon back in the cabin again.

"You made a quick jump outside, stranger," said the host. "Did your horses start and call you out?"

"Perhaps the coffee doesn't agree with him," put in the woman.

"O, yes, it does," I answered. "It is so stimulating that I just felt as though I must run about and exercise myself a little."

Mr. Priour was seated before the doorway and had seen everything that had occurred on the outside while the cabin proprietor and his wife had seen nothing, and I detected a subdued grin creep over my partner's face as I explained my hasty exit.

After all had drunk of the coffee, smoking was in order, and the lady of the house proved to be just as handy with a pipe as any of us. I thought none the less of her for this. She had as good a right to smoke as her husband, and manifestly enjoyed it as much as he. An hour or more was whiled away before we were ready to bid our entertainers an *adieu*, and after mounting our wagon and riding away, the jolly couple stood by the trail and watched us as long as we could see them. We felt refreshed by our pleasant call in spite of the coffee.

For several hours we drove slowly over the uninteresting prairie and I thought of how monotonous a life it must be for a family of two to live so far from neighbors. They could hardly be blamed for stopping strangers and conversing with them, or even setting traps for travelers.

CHAPTER XIV
IN THE CANEY BOTTOMS

About 4 o'clock p.m. we reached the bottoms of Caney Creek. The stream itself is extremely tortuous, and its course includes all points of the compass, even in the few miles that we saw of it. After driving a mile or two we crossed the creek by a rustic bridge, drove about two miles more and crossed again by a second bridge. This was rather provoking to my partner, for he had hoped to leave the bottoms before coming to camp, but after some scientific figuring, we made it that we were on the same side of the stream as before entering the timber. Hauling the wagon out by the side of the road we made arrangements to spend the night in Caney.

As soon as we were really anchored and had built a campfire, spectators began to congregate, and within thirty minutes we were completely surrounded. But the company was very tolerable, and their average state of civilization several degrees above those of the San Antonio River Settlement. These people were much concerned as to the nature of our business. Some took us for egg merchants, some for photographers, and still others for surveyors. When we told them of our business, they became much interested and volunteered information in regard to localities suitable for camping and hunting.

Lucid Directions

We inquired of our new friends the most direct route to Cedar Lake, and each one of our advisers made it his object to out-rival the others in his accuracy of minute details. To such an extent was this exactness carried, that at times their directions were ludicrous, and one would have thought they had studied the road expressly for the occasion.

"When yer go 'bout two mile from dat tree up dar by de ben' ob de road, ye'll come ter de bridge cross de kreak, an 's yer go ober dat, yer horses'll point right ober de top ob a hill. Go ober dis hill an 'bout half a quarter of a mile ye'll come ter a sto'. Dey is a pump by de sto' on de souf side, an de handle ob de pump point ter de right, but yer pass de pump on der lef han' an go right along. De man hab a close line in de yard by de sto' and—"

"Hole on dar," put in Number Twelve. "Dar's a mistake in de 'rections. De pump handle sometime point up in de air when de water pump up, an' dat close line been dun broke las' week."

"Now look here, strangers," chimed another. "Dese fellers, do de bes' dey can, but dey is wrong. De pump ain' on de souf side ob de sto', but de souf side ob de shed in de yard, an' de close line been done use for harness lines all der week an' put back for washin.' Dar's a stump by de corner ob de shed lef' by a tree dat de man cut down ter make a new wagon pole when de hosses broke it las' fall. Ye turn to de right off dar, an' foller de straight public road."

Being sifted from their unnecessary and confusing references, the directions given by these sable brethren agreed well with each other, and we considered them honest.

It was a relief to find someone who could inform us of the surrounding country without telling as big a lie as he could fabricate, and with one or two exceptions, these negroes were the only people we had met who had not thought it their duty to misinform us.

These inhabitants of Caney appeared the happiest of beings. Having lived at this place probably for the greater part of their lives, they knew of but little else and were contented. "Their greatest riches the ignorance of wealth."

At the first sign of daylight, the negroes were on hand again, and their numbers so great that our throats became tired of bidding them good morning. One boy of about sixteen years brought in a fresh snowy heron which he offered to sell for two bits, and as we were in want of such birds, we gladly paid him his price. The citizens of Caney made such flattering reports of the birds to be found in the bottoms, that we were persuaded to spend at least a part of the day in the place. Once our decision became known, all was confusion about the camp. Every negro boy who could muster a gun or dog, and many who had neither, stood ready to lead us into the land of mud and venom. Absalom had made friends of all the yellow dogs, as we had of their masters, and everything was favorable for a grand hunt through the gloomy swamp. The people did not appear to have thieving propensities, so we left our wagon and team in the care of an aged negro, and, headed by an army of black infantry shouting defiance, we plunged into the chaos of vines, brakes, briers, bogs and bayous.

Once in the swamp, our scouts spread out in all directions, and for a time, a charge of shot sent in any direction would have winged either a boy or a dog. Thinking so much noise would warn any birds of our approach, I watched my chance, and gradually worked myself away from the body of our co-laborers. I reasoned that Priour had already adopted this scheme, for he was nowhere within my sight.

I Fall into the Mire

The swamp was a most dismal one. The compact foliage of the many forms of vegetable life was dyed a deep black green; and the interwoven branches of the trees overhead shut out the light of day, so that it seemed as if we had been transported to some unearthly spot.

About a mile from our starting place, we came to a spot, several acres in extent, which was treeless and only grown by a scanty supply of annual weeds. This spot was lower than the surrounding land, and, seeing some freshwater shells a short distance within it, I laid my gun upon the ground and went after them. The edges of this cleared place were covered by a layer of leaves from the trees nearby, the layer diminishing in thickness as the distance from the trees increased.

My footing was quite firm at the start, but when within a few feet of the coveted shells, the layer of leaves broke through, and in an instant I was nearly waist deep in the mire. I struggled hard to regain the fragile crust again, but like ice, when a man has broken through, it gives way much easier when once a place is opened, and my labors seemed only to force me deeper into the mud. If I had only been web-footed, I believe I could have worked my way to the top, but drawing up one foot shoved the other down a like distance, and I made no more headway than if on a treadmill. In the midst of my herculean efforts, a young negro lad made his appearance, and halting on solid footing, shouted to me:

"Mister, mister, it be boggy in dar. Look out."

Hearing his voice, another lad rushed to the scene and lent his advice. "Look out dar, Mister. De bogs down dar sure. Doan go in dar too far, Mister."

I could find no time to make answer to these remarks, for in spite of my endeavors, I was still getting in deeper and deeper. It seemed as though something had me by the feet, and if they had been attached to a fifty-pound weight, they could not have dragged me down faster. Still the young negroes collected on the bank, and each and every one of them shouted to me that it was "boggy in dar." It was clear to me that I should never be able to get out unaided, and the spectators didn't know enough to do anything besides tell me it was boggy. When nearly up to my armpits in the viselike stuff, and all hope lost of ever getting out again, there was a fresh arrival on the land before me. This was a broad-shouldered adult negro, who, seeing my misery and danger, at once came to my rescue.

Aided by the boys, he quickly gathered enough logs to build a bridge out to me, and if ever I felt thankful, it was when I grasped one of the sticks which had been placed near me. Once having a hold of something firm, it was not such a difficult matter to work my way out, and I was soon on good footing, expressing thanks to the man who had actually saved my life.

The Devil's Mouth

"Dat's a purty narrer 'scape, boss; 'bout one minute mo' 'n yo pard neber seed you agin."

"Yes," I replied. "I know that. Why didn't some of these boys come help me?"

"We fought you's foolin' all de time," said a youthful spokesman. "Good golly, we fought eberybody know dat place, sure. Dat de Debil's Mouf."

"Yes, sah," said my deliverer. "Dat de Debil's Mouf, 'n many poor nigger git swallered up dar, too. Yah! yah! Look yer close!"

"Yes, look de close," chimed a dozen boys. "Yah! yah! yah! Ha! ha! He-yu! Hoo-oo-oo! Yi!"

My clothes were worth looking at, for I was mud from head to foot, and a soft, slimy, sticky mud at that. How I was ever to get clean again was a question, but as clothing dries quickly in Texas, I hoped some of the gluey stuff would fall off before night. I didn't want Mr. Priour to see me in such a dress, but I was some little distance from the creek, and hadn't seen as much of the swamp as I wished to, so I thought I would let my clothing clean itself by a natural process.

We went still deeper into the gloomy wood, doubled around the far side of the place where I had foundered, and took a course back toward the creek again. The Devil's Mouth is not the only bog-hole in the Caney bottoms, for during the tramp we found several others, which, according to the negroes, were "jes as sassy as de fust one." I had often been bogged before, but it did seem that the Devil's Mouth was the most "sassy" of any slough I had probed.

I wondered where my partner could be all of this time, but supposed that, like myself, he was enjoying the bottom's scenery in company with a troop of boys and dogs. It was nearly mid-day when we reached the bank of the stream again, which we did several miles below the place where we had camped. We returned the rest of the distance by the public road, and I saw the negro settlement in all its thriftiness. The crops were mostly of cotton and corn, and were skillfully cultivated. The negroes lived in small log cabins of their own construction, and were as happy as so many birds. Their wants were few and all easily satisfied, for the soil is rich and but little labor is required to harvest good returns.

But for its snakes, its bogs, and its tormenting insects, Caney would be a paradise and, as the people seem to be little concerned about any of these undesirable things, they might consider themselves in a Garden of Eden.

I Excite Levity

Every negro who saw me had some remark to make concerning the load of mud I was carrying about, for although it had dried considerably, there was enough left on my clothing to show every one that I had been bogged. My appearance was the occasion of such mirth among the natives that even the women could not refrain from going in ecstasy when I passed their dooryards, and my young companions were more than willing to give to each questioner the full details of my misfortune. If there had been but one boy I could have easily walked away while he was telling the story of how "de gemman got in de Debil's Mouf," but by the time I had outwalked the last one, the one further down would have finished his lecture, overtaken me, and been ready for his next audience.

"Hoo-ee! What de matter dat gemman's coat, he been in de bog? Yah-hoo!"

"Yah, he went in de Debil's Mouf fo' de shells dar, 'n' he go down to he shoulder. Good golly, we all ben' on 'n' bil' a bridge out dar fo' git him out. He mos' die, sho."

"Hoe-you-yah! What he wan' dem shells fo'? Dey ain' no good; been dead fo' years."

"He doan eat um, he carry um up Norf, he say."

"He-yah-yah! Dey jes's dead when he git um dar's dey be here. Dat man ain' got no brains. He good 'nough fo' Debil's Mouf. He-yah-hoo! Better lef him in dar sure 'nough."

During such conversations as this the women were too much pleased to think of keeping quiet, and they danced about in their yards or floorless houses in a very ungraceful style, some of them far overstepping the bounds of modesty and decency, in their anxiety to beat the earth with their flat feet.

If I had only known a by-path to our camp, or if I had had some extra garment to cover the dried mud on my clothes and person, I should have been happy. But there was no help for me, and I ran the gauntlet with as good grace as possible. The dread of meeting Mr. Priour in my muddy condition had by this time been much modified, for there was but one of him, and that one couldn't ridicule me half as much as each of a dozen negro women had already done.

As I neared camp, this feeling of shame left me entirely, for there was strong evidence that my comrade had fared no better in the bottoms than myself. Entering the small cleared spot where our wagon stood, I found the man bare-legged, lustily beating his pants against the butt of a tree, and the amount of dirt and dust circulating about him would have routed a sandblast. Priour's shirt had been drenched in mire and was as muddy as my own, and if he hadn't found the Devil's Mouth, he had found another place "jes' as sassy."

"What's the matter with your pants, hornets in them?" I asked.

"No. Not hornets but dog-gon'd Caney mud, and if I'm ever caught in this hole again you can shoot me on the spot."

"Did you get bogged?" I asked.

"No, I didn't get bogged, but I guess you did; you look as though you'd been dragged for an hour through the mire."

"O, no," I answered, "I stepped on a log and it bent and squirted the stuff up on me."

"Well," he replied, "you must have stepped on a breechloading steam-squirt-gun to do all of that. You ought to have saved that gun to put out fires with, or to drown bears a mile away."

"Well, how did *you* get so muddy?" I ventured to ask.

"O, I got muddy easy enough. You see, I killed a warbler, and when he fell, he struck the mud and it flew up on me in the same way that two-foot log bent when you stepped on it. I tell you, this is a queer country, and don't you ever step on a log again." Here the conversation stopped, but we were both wise enough to know that the half had not been told.

We Give a Show

After beating his pants until they were too pliant to stand alone, Mr. Priour backed out of his shirt and put that garment through the same course of treatment, while I, ever-ready to profit by his judgment, removed my clothing and kept time with his strokes on another tree. Admission to the clearing was free during this act, and before we were ready to put our raiment on again there were more spectators than I supposed could live in the settlement.

"Yah! yah! Hoo-oo! He got in de mud! He got he shirt all ober mud."

"Hoo-yaw! He got mud in he boot! He mud on de head."

"Go scrape dat mud out he eye dar."

"Look dem pants wine 'roun de tree. Hee! Yah! Hoo!"

"Git a hoe 'n scrape he legs dar!"

"Hoo! You! What he gal say, she see him now?"

Grand chorus: "Yah! Yoh! He!" "Who! Yah! Ho!" "Hi-yo! Hoo-yaw!" "Kee-ye-hu!"

So violent were the mirthful gestures, contortions and exclamations of these men and women that the contagion was irrepressible, and Priour and myself soon succumbed and laughed as heartily as was possible without the use of the African throat. Finally we were in our clothes again, when the audience became quieter, allowing us to converse with each other without shouting.

Taking account of stock we found that our morning's hunt had not been such a profitable affair as we had hoped it would be. We had several good birds, but no more than we had often obtained with much less labor. The remainder of the day was spent in skinning birds and answering dark-colored questions.

CHAPTER XV
IN WHICH I GO DOWN A WELL

The next morning we were on the road at an early hour, and after driving a mile or more, crossed the stream by another native bridge.

Near this crossing was the store which had been so accurately described by our recent friends. The clothes-line, pump-handle, etc., were just as they had been represented to us, and we knew that thus far we were on the right road.

Caney Store

We stopped to purchase a supply of grain for our team. There was no room in the building for storing corn, and the latter was kept in the field on the stalks just as it had grow the year before. This was an ingenious way of doing business. Instead of being lumbered up by a great pile of grain, all the merchant had to do was to send his customer into the field with a bag to make his own selection of quality and quantity. This grocer had another cute arrangement about his emporium. This was a short piece of hardwood log which was estimated to be just as heavy as a bushel of corn, and the latter was weighed by the proprietor's lifting first the log and then the grain, his judgment telling him when one about balanced the other. I will, however, give the grocer all due credit by stating that he allowed both Priour and myself to say when we thought enough corn had been put in the bag to equal the weight of his stick.

We saw about this place many other pieces of wood used for the purpose of dealing out the right quantity of other kinds of merchandise, and each log was labeled to indicate for what it was to be used. Thus one stick was marked "2-bits' worth of jerked beef," another, "4-bits' worth of hog grease," and others, "A day's work's worth of flour," "A pile of wood's worth of coffee," "A dozen good eggs' worth of tobacco," etc.

Shortly after leaving the Caney store we emerged from the bottoms and struck the unsettled country again. About a mile and a half from the bottoms we drove to the edge of one of the largest groves and took a tramp through it. Going nearly a quarter-mile within the growth I came to a somewhat open space which held ten or twelve post-oaks, and every tree of them held at least a score of nests of the great-tailed grackle. Some nests were hardly completed, while others contained one, two, three and four eggs each. These birds are torments to the farmers, and had their rendezvous been known in Caney, the grove would have resounded with the African gun until the last grackle had been executed. Climbing one of the trees I rescued sixty-nine eggs, all being within easy reach while standing in one position on a limb.

Journeying eastward, our way gradually became more and more surrounded by the wood until finally a path cut through brush and timber was the only way in which we could drive. Within this wood were numerous small clearings, all occupied by negroes who tilled the rich soil just enough to raise sufficient food for their large families, and, from appearances, the people spent the most of their time basking in the hot sun. Though they had such wretched surroundings and were probably unacquainted with food and clothing other than the very coarsest, they knew one of the luxuries of life that millions of people know not. This luxury was contentment, and on every face that we saw about these clearings could be read that one word.

To sit by the door of a low, rickety log cabin, and watch the gambols of a score of naked children playing in the dirt, was all the occupation the parents of these homes seemed to have. Timber at their very doors, and too little ambition to cut enough to repair their houses. Plenty of fertile soil waiting to be tilled and to produce good crops, and too little enterprise to clear it up. These people in their unlimited tranquility and perfect unconcern were truly enviable. They were so easily satisfied with what they did not have, that should one of them fall into the water, he would be contented to drown rather than try for the shore. Just how far contentment may extend without merging into laziness I do not know, and it would not make one whit of difference to these negroes which it was called, so long as they were enjoying the condition.

Taking the Census

"Hey, you!" shouted my partner to the proprietor of one of these hovels. "Whose children are all of these?"

"Dem my chillun, sah. I got de bes' lookin' flock ob chillun in de State ob Texas."

"What are you going to do with them all?"

"All gwine ter grow up lawyers, sah, sho."

"Why don't you go into your field and tend to your corn?"

"Corn grow jes same when I ain' out dar. Where yer goin' dat team, huntin' rabbits?"

"No. We're after birds."

"Birds! Good golly! What fo yer wan' birds? Rabbits better 'n birds. I likes rabbits."

"We want birds to look at when we get home."

"Hoo! Yah! Wan' birds ter look at! Yer neber git fat dat way. I eats my grub—lookin' at it, doan do me no good."

"Why don't you fix up your house, and keep your children dry when it rains?"

"Look he-ar, stranger. Dis my house an de ole woman say it good 'nough. Doan ax too many questions 'bout dis house."

"Yes, your house is good, but it needs a roof."

"Well, stranger. Dis house hab a ruf once, an' de win' blow it down an' kill one ob de chillun in de night."

"Why didn't you put it up again?"

"Stranger, I did put it up agin, an' de nex' night it come down an' kill de bes' boy I hab."

"Why didn't you keep putting it up again. I wouldn't be bluffed by a roof."

"Stranger, I keep puttid' dat ruf on fo' seben times an' it come down ebery night an' kill one de chillun. I dun git tired ob puttin' up dat ruf an' buryin' babies. I doan hab no more ruf on my house, sho."

"How many children have you got left after losing that seven?"

"I's got jes two more 'n Sam Carter's got."

"How many has Sam got?"

"I doan know zacly, but he ain' got so many's me by jes two 'an he ain' hab died but fo' ob dem since he ben here."

"Too bad you've lost so many children."

"Stranger, it am bad, but look he-ar, Sam Carter doan beat dis chile yet."

During this conversation the many children of the home, prompted by curiosity, had assembled about our team until we were completely encircled. Really, it looked as though some African asylum had been turned loose in the clearing, and we had to drive carefully for some distance to avoid crushing them under our wheels.

The Lake is Elusive

About noon we came to another plantation with its ruins of cotton gin and sugar-house. This place was smaller than the one at Caney, and not as nicely laid out. Near this place we drove over a bridge crossing a narrow stream of water, which we were informed was the lower end of the pond we were in search of. Turning to the left here we drove through the gateways of several pasture fences and entered the forest. We could pick a way for our wagon between the trees, and taking a course which we supposed would be convergent with the sides of the body of water, we drove until the wood became impenetrable by our team. Then we came to camp, supposing we were only a short distance from Cedar Lake.

We were now several miles from the bridge recently crossed, and as no water had been brought from there, I took a small tin pail and went for some of that liquid, while Mr. Priour busied himself in roasting coffee for our dinner. Starting off with a light heart I little knew what was in store for me. I thought the lake couldn't be more than a quarter-mile from our camp at the furthest, but after traveling twice that distance I began to wonder if there was water anywhere about us. The sun was shining brightly and I couldn't well lose my way, so I went further and further toward the visionary pond.

After traveling I should judge about two miles, I saw signs of daylight, and soon came to a clearing in which was situated a log hut. This didn't look much like a lake, but I wanted water, lake or no lake, and seeing no one about, I went to the door of this cabin. Here I was met by an aged negress who had undoubtedly never seen a white man before.

"Halloo, dar. What yer gwine do dat pail? Dis ain' no place fo' white man."

"I want to find the lake; can you tell me where it is?"

"What yer talking 'bout? What lake?"

"Cedar Lake."

"Cedar Lake?"

"Yes, Cedar Lake. Is it down this way?"

"G'way from here. I tell yer, dey ain' no such lake in dis country."

"Didn't you ever hear of Cedar Lake?"

"No, sah. I neber heard ob Cedar Lake afore. You's tryin' fool dis ole nigger. I set de dog on ye."

"I want some water in this pail; can I get some here?"

"What yer wan water fo?"

"To drink, of course."

"Dey ain' no water 'roun' here but de slough."

"Where do you get your water?"

"Out de slough where dem ducks be."

"That looks like dreadful dirty water."

"Dey ain' no mo' water 'roun' here dan dat 'less yer go down in der swamp to ole Bill Shephard's well."

"How far is that?"

"'Bout a mile. Go right down dar, an' yer'll fine it. Dey ain' nobody lib dar now, but de well dar jes de same."

How a person could habitually drink such water as was in the slough I could not understand. I had often drank as muddy water myself, but never when there was a possibility of getting better, and following the woman's direction I plunged deeper into the swamp, hoping to find Bill Shephard's well. All this trouble was more than the water was worth, but I didn't want to go back with an empty pail, and didn't mean to do so if I could find anything to put into it.

A walk of a little less than a mile through the gloomy wood brought me to a second clearing where I found the remains of a log cabin, and the well. This well was about twelve or thirteen feet in depth, was rickety and looked as though it was about ready to collapse. There was no provision for drawing water to the top, and no signs that the place had been visited by man for years.

The ground was covered with a luxuriant growth of creeping vines and shrubbery, and I caught a glimpse of many a shining snake sliding among the matted and tangled weeds. The place seemed to have been abandoned to beings vile quite some time ago.

I was just a little faint-hearted and felt like leaving the unearthly place at once, but three miles was too long a distance to tramp for nothing, and I resolved to visit the subterranean pool. Bracing my hands and feet apart as best I could, I cautiously descended this hole in the earth.

In a Hot Place

This was ticklish business, for the boards with which the cavity was lined and braced were in the last stage of rottenness, and certainly needed but a slight jar to provoke an avalanche. However, I soon reached the level of the water without accident, and stooping filled my pail to the brim. Pausing here for a moment, the thought came over me that it was going to be more difficult to ascend with a filled pail than it had been to descend with an empty one.

While I was turning this idea over in my mind, one of my feet lost its hold between two of the side boards, and in attempting to recover my equilibrium, I tore out from the side of the well a 96-chambered wasp nest of .38-caliber, and every chamber turned loose an able-bodied black warrior, armed to the teeth—or tail. These little fiends then assailed me from every quarter, and I was clearly at their mercy. My hands and feet were all in use and could not be spared a moment for fighting, for a blow from one of my extremities would certainly have disarranged all my accurately adjusted points of balance.

To do or not to do, that was the question—whether it were better to drop into the water and drown myself, and thus foil my enemies, or to try for the top of the well. I knew nothing of how deep the water might be. I wouldn't have been any better off in up to my chin than where I was, and dreading a bath in a pool which, I thought, very likely contained numerous species of animal life hostile to man, I gave up all thoughts of relief below. I had never thought that a person could keep sober while being stabbed by a drove of wasps, but my deliverance lay in my sobriety, and knowing this I deliberately climbed to the surface of the earth as though there was no such thing in the world as a poisoned javelin.

Like some yellow dog pelted with stones and tin cans, I paused not to avenge the many insults and injuries thrust upon me, but fixed my eyes upon the small square of daylight above; each sting received stimulating me to care and precision rather than disastrous haste. If it had been otherwise I would have gone back to the bottom a dozen times before being at liberty again.

Once on the level earth's surface I was myself again, and reckoning my gains and losses, found some eleven places in which the fiery black demons had done their work, three on my ankles, three on my wrists and hands, and five on my neck and face.

Strange as it may seem, the wasps made no attempt to injure me when once I was on top of the ground and, gazing back into the dungeon of torture now alive with the merciless venom-injectors, I breathed a sigh of relief and marveled that I had succeeded in getting out alive.

If I had been stung to insensibility, it is doubtful if Mr. Priour would ever have found me, and he merely would not have done so unless chancing to question the negro woman who had sent me here. With no guidance save the direction which I had seemed to take when leaving camp, a person hunting for me would hardly have found the clearing three miles within the swamp, for it was originally small, and at this time much overgrown with brush.

Fortunately I had not been stung near the eyes, and after applying a poultice of moist tobacco to each swelling for a few moments, I picked up the unspilled pail of water, and shouldering my gun took steps toward camp. Although the stings smarted much, I had a light heart, and the more I thought of the predicament in which I had been placed, the more I rejoiced at my deliverance.

I Afford Mirth

Following on my return the course which had taken me to the fountain, I soon reached the first clearing found on my way out, and as I approached the cabin the negress stood by the door in readiness to continue our conversation.

"Hey, dar!" she shouted as I drew near her. "Did yer fine any water down ter Bill Shephard's well?"

"Yes," I replied. "I found water and wasps, too. Do you see those stings on my face?"

"Yah! yah! yaw! Sting-bee on de mug! He! hah! who! Dat's too good," and gathering up her insufficient skirts, this woman danced a snatch of jig in honor of my punishment. "How yer git stung dar?" she continued. "By de side ob der well?"

"Yes," I replied. "I went down it, and was stung eleven times before I could get out. Did you know there were—"

"Hah! yah! he-you! Stung 'leben time in de well. He! hoo! Better took water out'n de slough. You uns feel better'n we uns, but de bees sting white man jes same as nigger. Hoo! hu! wee-haw!" and another hilarious jig was jigged on the shanty floor, while the upsetting of a rude table supporting an iron pot and several pieces of tinware lent an apt accompaniment to the uninspiring performance.

It was only too manifest that the aged woman was delighted at my misfortune, and in the midst of her violent emotions I slid out of the clearing, paying no attention to her final shout of: "Say, mister, which hurt de mos'? Seben or 'leben?"

In due time I reached our camp, having been away on the water hunt several hours. "Well, I'll be dog-on'd," said my partner. "I never expected to see you again. Absalom and I were just coming down to the lake after you. See any birds down there?"

"HAH! YAH! HE-YOU!"

"Yes," I replied. "I saw plenty of the birds that carry their spurs in their tails," and proceeding to explain my long absence I gently broke the news to Mr. Priour that there was no such body of water in Texas as Cedar Lake, and that we had been deceived by maps and by people stationed along our route for that purpose. I also informed him of how Rebekah, instead of furnishing water for ourselves and team, had sent me away into the wilderness to be stung to death. Mr. Priour was as much pleased at the narrative of the waspy onslaught as the negress had been, and laughed heartily at the souvenirs of the fray which I conspicuously carried on my face, hands and legs.

I could see nothing to laugh at in connection with my late experience, and by this time my face was swollen to such an extent that laughing would have been painful.

I didn't feel much like eating dinner, but drank a little coffee for my stomach's sake. My head was paining me quite severely, and feeling no more like hunting than eating I filled my ever-pacifying pipe, and lying under the shady trees, smoked my headache to the four winds. Mr. Priour was not quite satisfied with the result of my explorations and ridiculed me somewhat upon my failure to find the lake.

Mr. Priour Frees His Mind

"Now, I'll be dog-on'd if I don't show you how to find water," he said. "I've lived in Texas long enough to know water when I see it. There's a lake side of us, and when Ab and I find it I'll come back and lead you down there. Ha, ha, ha!" and accompanied by his dog the man left my presence.

My pains dispelled by the most-comforting tobacco I soon fell asleep and fought my waspy battle over again. It was late in the day when I awoke, finding myself bathed in a profuse perspiration and shivering with cold. The poison and nightmare together had sweated me, and collecting some dry sticks I mended the dying fire and seated myself by it.

I was soon warmed and restored, and taking my gun I stirred about enough to kill a few wrens and flycatchers. By dark Mr. Priour and Absalom had returned, and he was as disgusted with the place as I.

"Now, I'll be dog-on'd if this ain't the driest place I've struck yet. You was lucky to find wasps. I haven't seen even that kind of bird."

"Did you find the lake?" I asked.

"Find the lake! What lake? You didn't suppose I was fool enough to think there was any lake about here, did you?"

"I thought those negroes at Caney were telling us the truth," I answered.

"Telling the truth! Did you ever know a nigger to tell the truth? Dog-on them Caneyites. If I had them here I'd make them dig me a lake!"

"What was that water we crossed this morning if it wasn't a lake."

"What was it? Why, it was a slough where the niggers empty their wash tubs, of course. I could see the whole length of it from their bridge, and here we've drove five or six miles hunting for a Jack-o'-lantern, and them niggers all laughing at us. I'm going back there tomorrow and lay out a string of them that'll make a black streak a mile long when they're put endways."

After thus freeing his mind my partner felt easier, and I too. There was undoubtedly a Cedar Lake somewhere within a few miles of us. As it was, we had not even water for our supper. We were quite thirsty, but I did not hanker for drink enough to approach Bill Shephard's well again, and we concluded that a dry supper and breakfast would be on our bill of fare.

"Now, if we could only do like Absalom," said the dog's master, "we'd be all right, water or no water."

"Why, what does he do for drink?" I asked.

"He kills coons and sucks their blood. He killed two this afternoon and sucked them as dry's a bag."

"Then he isn't a dog after all, but a bloodsucker, is he?"

"No, he ain't a bloodsucker, but a blood extractor, dog-on him, and a keen one, too. I've seen him suck all the blood, flesh and bone out of a coon, and you couldn't find the place where he did it, either."

CHAPTER XVI
ABSALOM SHOWS ME THE WAY

Early the next morning, after the ceremony of a nominal breakfast, we attempted to make preparations for a hasty evacuation of the swamp. But we were to be disappointed, for Whitie some time during the night had broken his hitch-line and, with Gruya, had left our camp, probably in search of water. The horses could hardly be blamed for this, for the previous day had been hot and their labors hard, and they were as thirsty as we were. However, there was nothing for us but to hunt for them, and as every minute's delay was so much longer for us to be without water, we took different courses, and started at once.

After rambling through the wood in a zigzag fashion for two hours or less I found symptoms of moisture. The ground was somewhat spongy, and the leaves and brush underfoot were in places slightly damp. This discovery revived my spirits, for really I was much more interested in signs of water than of horse flesh. I was well satisfied that if the horses were found, Priour would be the lucky man, and going in whatever direction that seemed most juicy underfoot, I kept my eyes directed to the ground rather than among the trees.

Within another half-hour I came to a spot which was humid enough to wet my shoe when I jumped heavily, and I conceived the idea of digging a little well of my own. Cutting a proper sized stick, I shaved one end down to a thin edge and began operations. A half-hour's patient toil thus resulted in my having a two-foot well with a few inches of water in the bottom. This latter was much roiled and muddy, but fashioning a dipper of some leaves, I drank enough to quench my thirst a little, and then concluded to wait a little while for the dirt to settle. After a time the water in my reservoir was in good drinking condition and I drank my fill.

Thinking my partner must surely have found the horses by this time, I left my well and wandered back toward the spot I had left several hours before. I wasn't thirsty now and the swamp didn't seem near as dreary as when I started out on the horse hunt, and if water could have been found near us, I wouldn't have minded spending another day in the place.

I had pictured my partner waiting for my arrival, the team harnessed, and all in readiness for our departure. But as I neared the spot wherein we had camped I was confused at the scene before me, for something surely had happened. The wagon was gone, as were all of our traps, and the only visible thing that had come with us was our dog. Poor Absalom; he lay upon the rough ground, beneath a great log which some one had thrown across his prostrate body. At my approach the animal whined piteously, showing that life was not yet extinct, but owing to the weight of the log he could make no motion whatever.

I Conjure Up Terrors

Here was a mystery indeed. Had someone foully murdered my companion, stolen the team, and left the dog thus imprisoned to die of starvation? Perhaps, now, I thought, the assassins are lurking about, waiting to get a shot at me, and instinctively grasping my gun firmly I slid behind a tree and cast searching glances across the tiny space before me. I could see no signs of a struggle, and I knew my partner was not the man to be killed without one, so I reasoned that the murder must have been committed outside the camp. Then it came across me that probably the ruffians supposed Priour to be alone, and that I had been spared through their ignorance of my presence in the swamp. This was something of a relief, and my long stiffened hair began to relax a little.

Of course, the murdered man's body was somewhere within a few yards of me, and it would be my sacred duty to see that it had a decent burial. I knew, too, that I should take steps to inform the authorities of the whole train of circumstances, and if possible have the guilty persons brought to punishment. All these thoughts passed through my mind in rapid succession, while I was still eying everything sharply from behind my tree.

All at once I caught sight of a bit of paper hanging from a bush and pierced by the stub of a broken twig. My confusion returned, but bracing up my nerves, I cautiously came from my hiding and seized the note. As I read it, my fear vanished as suddenly as it had come, for there in the handwriting of J. M. Priour was:

> You lazy fool! Do you suppose I'm going to wait here all day for you and choke to death? I'm going where there's water and you can come when you get ready. I'll leave Absalom for you, and he'll show you the trail I took.

How clear everything seemed to me then, and what a relief it was to know that my partner was alive, and that I wouldn't have to go back to Corpus Christi alone and report his death. I was as happy as when just out of Bill Shephard's well. Thoughtful man, Mr. Priour. He wanted to leave Absalom to lead me out of the wilderness, and being minus a piece of line, he had rolled a log on the animal to hold him until my arrival. This was a little rough on the dog, but as his skin was tough and quite empty, there was nothing to be much injured by the stratagem.

For once in my life I did feel a little kindliness toward Absalom, for he was going to pilot me safely to my companion, and I partially forgave him some of the many charges I had against him. How long he had been pinned to the ground I knew not, but I believed it could hot have been more than an hour or so.

I grasped one end of Absalom's burden and raised it from its resting place. With a yell of delight, like some schoolboy turned loose after an hour's delay, the guide who was to lead me out of the solitude made a dash through the brush, and within three seconds was out of sight and sound. This was something unexpected, for had I anticipated any such action I could easily have made sure of his companionship by the use of a flexible withe. His sudden desertion more than counteracted all the nice things I had so recently thought of him. The only course for me now was to follow the trail myself, and as Priour was getting further away every minute, I left at once.

Guiding Signals

Our wagon was quite heavy, and as a course through the timber must be anything but straight, I knew I could easily overtake the team. I had little difficulty in following the trail, for it was fresh and Mr. Priour had never been known to turn out for any tree, stump or log that he could drive over, or any bayou, slough or gully he could drive through. I did not try to follow the wagon at every turn it had made, but by looking ahead some little distance I could see trees that had had their bark scraped off by the overriding of our axle, and with the help of these blazes, made rapid progress. Thirty minutes outside camp I fell in with our stew-pot.

This circumstance I interpreted to mean that Absalom had reached his master and that the latter had thrown the utensil off to let me know—if I found it—that I was on the right trail, so picking up the article I took it along. Ten minutes after this I came across the tail-board of the wagon, together with, the iron rod by which it was kept in place. This I interpreted to mean that when I found them I was to know that I was still on the right trail, and I took them also along with me. Shortly after this ingenuous communication I found our lantern and a collection of loaded shells, about fifteen or twenty in number, which told me as plain as so many words that I was yet in the wake of our wagon, and I gathered these things in. I was loaded now, and sincerely hoped my partner wouldn't send me any more cipher dispatches.

For fear of finding more of our goods with which to burden myself, I partially closed my eyes, keeping them open just enough to steer clear of trees. But this artifice availed me nothing, for I soon stumbled over a bag of corn. This was consoling, as I was then certain that I had not been led out of my way. It would have pleased me better though if I had found something lighter. Forbearance had ceased to be a virtue, and I skillfully climbed over this sack and continued my way.

I was momentarily expecting to find a dead horse or wagon wheel, for Priour was determined that I should not lose myself and would sacrifice anything for my guidance. If he had only knocked Absalom in the head and made a milestone of his remains, the sight of it would have well repaid me for my long walk, but I knew that the dog would be the last thing to be left for me.

All Well that Ends Well

The next thing I fell in with was words—words from the rich musical tongue of my partner. I could not see the man, but the sounds that were wafted to my ears were: "Now, I'll be most everlastingly dog-on'd if that tail-board ain't got unhung! Here's the dad-gon'dest scrape I ever got blasted into! Half the whole load gone and strung way back here for a mile, and if I ever get hold of that feller's neck that kept me waiting so long, I'll wring it off if I die for it!"

Why I was thus to be maimed I knew not. I had certainly I done my full duty in making a pack-horse of myself, and so hazarding my neck I carried my burden into the presence of Mr. Priour. He did not fly at me nor did he make a grab at my neck, but was as pleased to see the stray articles coming in as I was to drop them.

"Well," he said. " How do you like coming on behind afoot, I and what was you doing down in the swamp so long?"

"I was hunting the horses, of course."

"Hunting the horses! Well, you couldn't see a horse if he had his arms around your neck. I found them animals ten minutes after leaving camp, and yelled my throat sore for you to come in, and besides that, I waited an hour for you. Ain't you thirsty?"

"Of course I am. That's why I was so anxious to get out of that place, and hunted so long and hard."

"I wouldn't give very much for your hunting. Next time I won't leave my dog for you."

"Well, if you ever do leave him again he'll stay there till he dies. What good was he to me?"

"What good was he! Well, if it hadn't been for him you'd been groping around down there yet. He befriended you and you needn't blackguard him."

During this conversation the tail-board, lantern and other articles had been transferred to the wagon, and after the bag of corn had also been brought up, we mounted the load and were away.

The highway once found, we made good time, and within a few minutes had pulled up by a negro cabin to drain a well and cool the throats of ourselves and horses.

CHAPTER XVII
A CANINE SPOOK

By the middle of the afternoon San Bernard Creek appeared, and driving a short distance out of the road we camped in the swampy bottoms. Although we had passed many cabins on our way, there were few of them near this stream. But if the settlers kept away from the creek, their dogs did not, and each inhabitant of the settlement was represented about our wagon by one of these animals. Long, yellow, lank and hairless, these four-footed denizens flocked about us as though a part of our own family, and, figuratively, Absalom took each of them by the hand and gave him a hearty welcome to the hospitality of our camp.

Like many people who had called upon us, these dogs could take no hint that they were not wanted, and in several instances the proverbial kick was attempted in order to keep them from overrunning us entirely. They were, however, familiar with such treatment and could dodge a stroke of the foot by a single motion of the body which would invariably leave the animal in the place and position he was before.

Quicker than Sight

Mr. Priour tried to punish one of the dogs which had his nose in our stew pot. Several vigorous kicks were given in rapid succession. To me, standing a short distance away, it appeared as if the man's foot went right through the body of the animal, but the dog did not remove his nose from the dish nor did my partner's foot meet with any resistance. Whether the trained beast dropped flat upon the ground, allowing the intended blow to pass over him, or leaped high in the air above the danger, I could not tell, for the motion was too quick to follow with the eye.

"Well, now, I'll be dog-on'd," said the unsuccessful kicker, "that's the spookedest cuss that ever stole ham. It wa'n't never meant for him to be killed, and we couldn't do it if we tried. Now, you hear my words."

"Why couldn't we kill him? I don't believe he could dodge a charge of shot."

"Well, I wouldn't kill that dog now for a million skunk skins."

"Why not?"

"Why not! Why, I tell you, he's some spiritual descension, and what's more, he didn't, dodge my foot either."

"Yes, he did. You didn't strike him."

"I know I didn't strike him."

"Then he must have dodged you."

"No, he didn't dodge me."

"What did he do then?"

"He just ghosted every time; now, I'll be dog-on'd if I don't know it, and I'm going to keep him along with us for good luck."

"He dodged your foot, for I saw him slide under it."

"No, you didn't see him slide under it. I'm no elephant, I know, but when my foot starts, it generally gets there except in spooks. I tell you, that dog just all goes into spook when he wants to, and you might as well strike at your shadow with a club."

An Expert on Spooks

"I don't believe in spooks."

"Well, what of that! I knew a man once that didn't believe in bulls till he had a two-foot horn run through him, and was carried around on the bull's head for a week, then he just begun to believe in bulls."

"Were you ever tackled by a spook?"

"No, but I've known them to scare a man to death who might just as well been horned by a bull."

"Well, did you ever see a spook?"

"Yes, I've seen a spook!"

"Where was it?"

"Where I was living on the Aransas River."

"What was the spook doing?"

"It cut around as though 'twas crazy; kept running and ramming into the fence, and brought up there kersmack every time. I thought once 'twas going to knock the boards all down."

"What did it look like?"

"Looked like a big white goose."

"Did anybody around there keep geese?"

"Yes, the man that lived nearby had a whole pen full of them."

"Wasn't that a goose you saw?"

"No, 'twas a spook."

"Why didn't you run it down?"

"I did."

"Did you catch it?"

"Of course I did. Did you ever know me to let a thing go when I once doubled down to get after it?"

"What did it look like after you'd caught it?"

"Looked like a goose just as it did before."

"What did you do with it?"

"Picked the feathers off and had it for dinner next day. That's what I did with it after I wrung its neck."

"You stole a goose, that's what your spook was."

"No, 'twas a spook; but I tell you what, it looked and tasted so dog-on'd much like a goose that most anybody but me'd been deceived. But I took it for a spook when I first saw it, and I wa'n't no such fool as to change my mind just because it had feathers; and besides there ain't any law against stealing spooks."

"I guess that was the same kind of a spook this dog'll prove to be; one with something to it."

"Well, don't kill that dog anyway, he comes near enough a spook."

This settled the question on the champion dodger, and he was allowed—during his new friend's presence—various privileges refused other and less active visitors. We took a short stroll about the camp, and were lucky enough to shoot a few yellow squirrels which would make a nice stew for our supper, which proved to be the best meal we had eaten for many a day. Absalom got none of it nor did the other dogs, not even our new acquisition, now christened "Dodger." We had by this time discovered that this latter reinforcement was built something like other Texan dogs—of skin and air principally. We had also discovered that a large and sweeping bush was a much better article for defending the camp than a club or foot, and we kept a dozen of the former weapons lying about camp, available for immediate use.

After a long evening our tent was spread upon the ground, and surrounded by a circle of canine guards, a dozen strong, we turned in for the night.

CHAPTER XVII
I AM LOST AGAIN

We were early astir, and with the help of our many dogs we secured several more yellow squirrels. We did not quite like the appearance of the neighborhood and thought it best that one should remain with our things. We had caught glimpses of several dusky faces behind the trees, and as no one had called upon us it looked as though the spies were only waiting for us to go before making the camp a visit.

Finally it was decided that Priour should remain on duty, and, followed by three or four yellow dogs, Dodger included, I shouldered my gun and struck out for a ramble up the creek. Birds were wanting, but the swamp was worth inspecting, and I wound my way among the trees for miles and miles. For every bird that was absent nine snakes were present, but as they were living in a place of no earthly use to mankind, I could not fume very much about their monopoly. The dogs did not mind them often, and I tried to be as tolerant as my guides.

I had been too much interested in studying nature in all her uncouthness to pay any attention to the course taken, and when ready to retrace my way toward camp, I first noticed that the sky was clouded and the sun invisible. I had not the slightest idea of the direction of either the highway or creek, for I had seen nothing of the latter since my start in the morning. It was now several hours since I had left my partner. The dogs had stuck fast to me all the morning, and my next move was to try and send one of them away, hoping he would thereby show me the way I should go. Finding this useless, I accepted the only alternative and wandered aimlessly about in the swamp. I did not hurry myself any, indeed I consumed much more time in going over a given space than was needful. Not knowing whether I was diminishing or increasing the distance to camp, I reasoned that if the latter, the slower I went the better.

Many times before when so situated as to be uncertain just what move to make, I had asked myself the question: "What would Mr. Priour be likely to do if in the same predicament?" and as a mental answer to such a question had always helped me to act, I now inquired of myself what course my partner would pursue if in my place. The thoughts thus developed were: First, it would be very un-Priour-like to get into such a scrape; second, if he should by chance lose himself, he would guess what course would lead him out, and ninety-nine times out of a hundred that guess would be exactly right; and third, if by any possible chance he should not guess right, he would lose no flesh worrying about it, but graciously lie down and sleep three or four hours waiting for something to turn up.

I had by this time tramped enough to be satisfied that I had more than covered as much distance as I had been from camp, and following the dictates of Priourism I lay down, hoping something would happen within twenty-four hours at the most. The dogs seemed to concur and they, too, lay upon the damp ground within easy speaking distance of me.

Mr. Priour Guards the Camp

I had not long to wait for something to happen. I had not lost myself, but was beginning to doze when I heard something. That something was the report of a gun, and in an instant I was on my feet. I knew a gun would not be out hunting alone, and keeping the dogs as near to me as possible, I quietly made my way in the direction of the sound.

Within a few minutes the gun kindly sent another report through the wood, and cautiously following this up, I soon beheld the bearer of the weapon in the person of J. M. Priour, who had not thought it entirely safe to leave the camp unprotected.

Not wishing my partner to see me, I stepped noiselessly and shadowed him. The dogs seemed to know what was wanted of them and crept behind me as though approaching some timid game.

For ten or fifteen minutes Mr. Priour walked about a clump of heavy trees, and then took a bee line away from them. Following for a half-mile or more, I saw him enter our camp, and after waiting about five minutes I, too, entered camp, but from an opposite direction.

"Halloo! What'd you see up the creek?" asked the man.

"I didn't see much but snakes. What'd you see?"

"What'd I see! I haven't left camp yet—too many coons sneaking round."

"I thought I heard somebody shooting about half a mile up the creek," I answered.

"Some woolly nigger hunting squirrels," promptly replied my partner.

"How did you get those birds?" I asked, for the man had two summer redbirds, apparently quite fresh.

"O, them's some Absalom brought in," he replied. "I tell you, that dog's a snooker and a wiry one, too! When he can't find game, now there ain't any game around. He clim' a tree and caught one of them right on the wing and the other one he stole."

This explanation I did not criticise, for as long as nothing had been stolen by the bushrangers, I had no fault to find.

It was now past mid-day, and as hunting here was unremunerative, we ate a long lunch, and lying upon the ground lazed away the time until darkness was upon us. Dodger was plainly anxious to be a permanent part of our caravan, and as he was so attentive to us, we determined that night that if practicable, we would smuggle him off in the morning, and that he should share Absalom's responsibility as camp fiend. After deciding just how this could be done, we spread ourselves under the trees for the night.

Just at daybreak the next morning we were suddenly called to our senses by a pouring rain, and speedily turning out, we pitched the tent and stacked our goods within it. It poured and poured, and as our conglomerate covering shed water no better than a damp sponge, everything was finally drenched.

Absalom Foils Us

Three hours from the advent of the storm the sun was shining brightly in the east, and dragging our reeking stores to a more open space, we spread them and ourselves to dry. By the middle of the forenoon we were ready to load up and hunt for a livelier country. Emptying one of our packing boxes we turned it upside down over Dodger, making a cage for him in the bottom of the wagon, and with this box as a cornerstone, we piled on our weather-beaten luggage and pulled out of the swamp to the public road and the ferry across the San Bernard.

This ferryboat was nearly twice as long as it was wide, and looked as though every voyage it made might be its last. The owner of the ferry lived over his store at the water's edge, but employed a negro to manage the boat. We had hoped to make a quick run across the narrow creek and be out of danger of losing our new dog, but the fates had decided otherwise.

Absalom was the Benedict Arnold. He knew we had contraband goods aboard that wagon, and what was more, he suddenly became jealous of such goods and refused to step his foot on the boat. He did not mean to play second fiddle to any San Bernard dog, nor was he going to have our affections alienated by the alien. He could stand a deal of slander and abuse, but he could not stand this.

Mr. Priour coaxed and whistled, pleaded and cursed, but Ab was immovable. His eyes pictured the expression: "I'm no fool, Priour, I ain't going aboard of that boat till I make trouble for you. I'm willing to be starved to death and lied about, but I'll be dog-on'd if I'm going to stand this."

Finally another stratagem was decided upon to get the animal aboard—Priour and myself would corner him and make use of our strength and agility. We would run him down if necessary, for time was the all important thing with us now; negroes were beginning to collect, and we knew not at what moment there might be signs of life at the bottom of our loaded wagon.

A dozen of the dusky spectators volunteering their services, we formed a crescent of ourselves, and soon had the contrary cur surrounded on all sides but next the water, and it was at this period that he got in his evil work. First he began to whine, then to cry and yelp, and as quarters became closer, his cracked voice broke into a string of howls and snarls after the style of some wild beast at bay. Soon there were return howls like the reflexion of sound. These latter sounds were heartrending to Priour and myself. They were like death knells, for they came straight from the box in the rear of our wagon. A drowning man will catch at a straw, and somehow, it came into both our minds that the only possible salvation for us would be to convince the black host about us that Absalom's voice was really being reflected.

"Hear the echo! Hear the echo!" shouted Priour as a gust of muffled yelps came from the dog cage.

"Yes, hear the echo!" I cried.

"Hear my voice echo!" yelled Priour as he raised a howl that would have split a cord of wood into toothpicks. The echo answered every time, but it was not an exact echo. It was always different from the first sound and continued with fresh eruptions as though it had been wound up and touched off.

Dodger is Rescued

The negroes began to look wise while Priour and I, driven to desperation, launched forth new essays on the wondrous echo. But it was in vain. It was in vain that we made all kinds of unearthly noises and burst the veins of our faces and throats in doing it. We could not hide the source of that diabolical echo.

"Hol' on boss! Hol' on dar!" said one of the wicked negroes. "Dat ain' no jecko. I ain' no fool nigger; dat jecko in de wagon an' I know de soun'. Dat my dog, boss, suah."

Priour looked savage. "What you talking about, you fool!" he shouted. "Don't you know what echo is? You might just as well run after your shadow as after that noise. I never saw a bigger fool in my life."

"Hol' on, boss," came the reply, "I doan wan' no trouble heah, but dat my dog you dun got in de wagon, suah. I miss dat dog las' night."

"Well, how came your lousy whelp in there anyway? If I'd known he was there I'd thrown him in the river, and you after him. How came he in there, I say?"

"Hol' on, boss! I doan know how he came in dar; he slip roun' awful sly, dat dog do. Yah! yah! yah!"

"Ye, ya, hoo!" "Yo, he, how!" "Bar, he-yu, wah-ha!" chimed a dozen black throats.

Our scheme had failed, and the only thing now for us to do was to unpack the load and liberate our prisoner. This we soon did, Priour all the while wondering aloud: "How did the cuss get under that box without being seen?" and the negroes' eyes sparkling asparkle that said: "I know how he dun got dar; he dun got put dar."

There was great rejoicing when Dodger was with his brethren again, and the whole incident was but confirmatory of the expression: "Might makes right." But we had done our duty by the dog anyway. We had tried to emancipate him from slavery, and even though our attempts were futile, we felt a throbbing conscience say: "Noble undertaking, reward shall be thine."

During all of this dog business our wagon and team had been on the boat, and Absalom, now as gentle as a kitten, was seized by his master and thrown aboard as though an object of dreadfully little value. Four bits being delivered to the ferry captain, our vessel was soon in motion, and we both felt that the sooner we were out of sound of the tumultuous negroes the easier we would feel.

We Sail Down the River

On the far side of the creek there had been at one time a landing of plank, but this had long been out of repair, and as the bank was boggy, the raft-like boat must be driven with some force in order to slide up the slimy ridge and beyond the more pudding-like mire.

Complying with the manager's request to "gib a lif' an' sen 'er up de bank," Priour and myself seized the rotten line and "gib a lif'" most too sudden for our own good. The aged rope was not prepared for any but the mildest strain, and as it parted, the leaky scow swung around lengthwise the stream and, with the current as a source of power, headed for the Gulf of Mexico.

Instantly there was a great uproar both from our captain and the crowd ashore. The stream was not a swift one, but moved us along about as fast as a man would walk, and this motion was enough to scare the one negro about half out his wits, while the mob on the bank was jubilant at our misfortune. Priour and I had made ourselves somewhat unpopular, and though it was a delight for the negroes to see us going toward the Gulf, they were solicitous for the welfare of their African companion.

"Jump in de riber, Pete; jump in de riber 'n swim out; let dem fellers go out de sea!" "Swim for de sho', Pete; swim for de sho'!" "Pile out, Pete; we pull yer out de water!" "Pete! Pete! Come on de sho'; doan go wid dem fellers own de sea!" and like advice was hurled at poor Peter from the crowd that followed us on the bank.

So much advice Peter could not refuse to follow, and with a cheer of encouragement from his friends, he plunged into the stream and quickly swam to the shore.

Once the ferryman was safe, the negro picnic actually began. These fellows had been somewhat afraid of Priour while we were on shore, but now there was no probability of another meeting, they became defiant, and, walking abreast of us as far as the thick brush allowed, made very unpleasant remarks for our hearing: "Hey, dar; come back dat boat!" "Come back dar 'n steal nudder dog 'fo' yer go down de Gulf!" "What de price sail down de sea on dat boat, Cap'n!" "Hol' on, dar. Doan yer wan' a pilot down de riber?" "Bar, yah, yah!" "Ye, he,he-yo!" "Hoo-oo-oo!" "Blow de whistle, Cap! Blow de whistle!" "*Hoo*-hoo!"

The boat was not long in getting down where the stream was flanked by an impenetrable growth of brush and briers, and then we were free from further insult.

There was no pole on board which could be used to shove the craft ashore, and not much for Priour and myself to do but sing "A Life on the Ocean Wave," and we did not feel much like that. I was thankful that my partner did not lie down and go to sleep. I did not want to be left in full charge of the boat, and so I kept my tongue continually rattling to keep my shipmate from hunting a bunk and turning in. Had I not done this, most likely the man would have slept until we were twenty miles out to sea, and then only awaked to ask if dinner was ready, or if Absalom was safe.

Bound for the Gulf

"How far do you suppose it is from here to the Gulf?" I asked.

"How do you suppose I know?" he returned, as he began to load his pipe with tobacco. "It may be two miles and it may be two million, I'm going to have a good smoke on the way down anyway."

"But I don't want to go to the Gulf this way."

"No more do I, but what are you going to do about it?"

"Can't we run the box in to the shore?"

"Well, suppose you stick your legs over behind and play you was a steam paddle. I'll be Cap'n 'n' yell at you 'n' tell you where to head her for."

"Ain't you going to try and do something about getting out of this scrape?" I asked in a high voice.

"Yes," came the moderate reply. "I'm going to get this dog-on'd pipe agoing, 'n' everybody that sees the smoke'll think we're a steamboat 'n' I'm the chimney."

"I don't think this is anything to joke about."

"No more do I, but don't you go into a fit. I wa'n't built to fret, and dog-on'd if I'm going to spill my temper over an excursion down the San Bernard. What's this creek amount to anyway? I could wind the whole blarsted thing up on my finger and make a toy squirt-gun of it."

"Yes, but it'll get wider by and by; this thing wouldn't hold together five minutes on the Gulf."

"Well, now, we ain't going to the Gulf, or to Californi', or Mexico; something'll turn up by and by 'n' we'll go ashore where there's a better landing than at them niggers'. Before we go to the Gulf I'll take my hat and bail this river all out."

Mr. Priour had no intention of worrying himself into a fever, so I gave up fretting myself, and we just drifted with the current, all the time waiting for something to turn up. This something appeared in its own good time. A mile and a half below the place where the negro mob had halted, the stream was narrowed by a projecting bank, and as good luck would have it, this projection caught one end of our raft, which, swinging around crosswise the stream, drifted diagonally toward the opposite shore. Seeing this, Mr. Priour and myself made ready for action, and when the huge trough had entered shallow water we sprang overboard, and keeping hold of the vessel's sides for support, paddled toward land until the ship's bottom grounded in the soft mud. Sure enough, this landing proved to be

BOUND FOR THE GULF

a better one than that by the public road two miles above. The shrubbery was dense and the ground low and wet, but we had little trouble in working the boat up over the miry bank, and our hatchet soon cleared a passage for the team.

After all our property was safe on shore, Mr. Priour cut a pole and shoved the boat well out into the stream, and five minutes later it rounded a bend in the creek and passed from sight.

"There," said my companion, "if them dirty, woolly, black devils ever get that boat they'll have to come further 'n' this for it."

"I suppose there'll be trouble when the owner finds his boat is gone."

"Well, if I was the owner there wouldn't only be trouble, but there'd be a yeller coon hanging from every tree on this creek."

"The coons didn't lose the boat."

"Well, they might just as well; they cut the rope and sent us down here in the swamp, and I'm going to advertise them."

We now had a task before us indeed. Our object was to strike the public road about a mile from the ferry crossing, and taking a course divergent from the San Bernard, we wormed our way through the snarly bottoms, our wagon creaking and groaning over its rough usage from the trees, gulleys and hummocks. After a two-hour struggle with the swamp wilderness, we reached the highway and turned in the direction of Brazoria.

The early morning rain had left the road in a sticky condition, and our progress was nearly as slow as while in the swamp.

During the drive we killed a few beautiful specimens of hooded warblers and saw hundreds of vireos, titmice and flycatchers.

CHAPTER XIX
IN WHICH I HAVE A VISION

By the middle of the afternoon we had reached the small town of Brazoria, situated on the bank of the Brazos river, and after visiting a store and purchasing a supply of the everlasting crackers, we started for the mouth of the river, twenty-one miles away. The road lay parallel with the stream and was through the same dark and gloomy swamp we had gone over in the morning. There were negro settlements all along the way, and from the inquisitiveness of the people, one would suppose they had never seen a loaded wagon before. "What kine o' layout does yer call dat?" "What yer goin' de mouf de riber for?" "Is yer gwine ter bil er railroad?" "What yer got in all dem boxes?" and many other questions of a like nature were shot at us from nearly every negro house.

The bank of the river was too steep for our horses to descend and we were anxious to find a place where we could water them before coming to camp. About six miles from Brazoria it was beginning to get dark. We asked a negro if there was other water near us and he replied: "Dey ain' no water fer miles but de riber."

We decided to camp at once and bring water from the river for our team. Driving our wagon from the road into the edge of the timber, we prepared to make a night of it fifteen miles from the Gulf. The swamp was damp and fairly alive with insects of countless varieties—fleas, ticks, spiders, scorpions. We slept with these creatures, of course. We could not leave them and they would not leave us. As was my custom, I lighted my pipe after supper and lay down to enjoy a good smoke, but had been in the horizontal position less than ten minutes, when feeling a sharp sting upon my chest, I put my hand within my shirt and dragged forth a great spider. This animal was of a brick color. The stung spot swelled and pained me during the whole night. Mr. Priour slept as sweetly as a babe in the cradle, but he was toughened to these bedfellows while I was not.

I kept my pipe going during the most of the long time, and had it not been for that universal antidote—tobacco—I should have been driven to insanity long before daylight. I was glad enough when I could see to move about among the trees, and I took a long stroll in the morning before my partner had opened his eyes. After breakfast we spent a half-hour or less in bringing water from the river for our horses as we had done the evening before, and when each animal had drunk our small tin pail three or four times full, we harnessed up and started on our way again.

It would have been just as easy for the man we saw the night before to have told us the truth as to have told a lie, but he had preferred the latter for reasons known only by the Texan negro, and we had driven less than a mile when we came to a pond of water as clear and pure as any man need to care for.

"That's all you can tell by a Texas nigger," said my partner. "You can depend on their lying every time. I believe a nigger'd go without his breakfast any morning just for the sake of lying and saying he wasn't hungry."

"Well, I don't know as I blame them any for that; if I had to live in such a cursed country as this I'd lie every chance I could get, just out of spite."

"They don't do it out of spite, but because it goes with a black hide. We had a nigger at Papalote once that hadn't told the truth for ten years. Then we gave him a coat of white paint and he told the truth then just as long as that paint stayed on. When the black began to show through a little, he began to lie a little, and when the paint had all worn off, he told just as big lies as ever. We had to dock him a dollar a month on his wages to buy paint to keep him from lying."

Late in the day we reached the small settlement of Quintana at the mouth of the Brazos, and about one mile from this place we came to camp on the Gulf shore.

Texas Mosquitoes

We had hoped to find a place where we would be free from attacks of pernicious insects, but if the number of species was less, the number of individuals was many times greater than in the swamp where we had passed the preceding night. Extending back several miles from the Gulf coast is a tract of low marshy land. The grass here is coarse and stout, and it was no exaggeration to say that mosquitoes were ten times as thick as they were at Texana, and they were thicker there than at any place I had ever seen before. Every step in this grass drove up thousands of them, and sixteen pair of hands would have been needed to keep them clear of one's face. They were the sauciest of their kind, and a hundred of them striking a man's face at one time would bore it full of holes as quick as a charge of No. 12 shot. Before we had fairly caught on to their brutal butchery, they had painted both Priour and myself with our own blood.

We had an hour yet of daylight, and felt that during that time it was our duty to make some preparation for a peaceful night's sleep. Our tent had known too much of rough usage to be tight, and would offer no obstruction to the winged enemy, so we studied up a scheme which we thought worthy of trial.

There was an abundance of driftwood on the shore, hundreds of cords which had been accumulating for many years. As near as we could see there was one unbroken line of logs, boards, timber and brush piled up in confusion, and it was to this wood that we looked for protection. Pitching tent on the level sand, we went for the logs. Backload after backload we carried to camp, and at dark our bedchamber was surrounded by a circle of combustibles twenty-five or thirty feet in diameter and several feet high. The horses and wagon were left outside, but Mr. Priour insisted upon Absalom's being within the fortification. There was no need of this, for the dog clearly had the advantage of us. He could draw his head and extremities within his shell like a turtle and bid defiance to any of the insect tribe, but his master's wishes were honored nevertheless.

Smoking Them Out

Our circle of firewood was dry and easily lighted, and we were soon surrounded by smoke and flame through which no insect could pass. We were safe from mosquitoes, and although somewhat choked by hot air and clouds of blackness from the fire, we made coffee and ate a hearty supper. By the time this meal was finished we were feeling uncomfortably warm, for the air was close and sultry even without artificial heat, and with the heat it was decidedly worse. Going in-side the tent we lay down and tried to smoke our pipes. I suppose we did smoke them, but there was too much competition from the logs for us to be certain of that fact. The wood-smoke pounced in through the tears and seams of our tent in clouds that were both blinding and suffocating and, as we could not see across the little space even by the aid of our lantern, our only knowledge of whether we were smoking tobacco or not was the fact that the pipes finally became empty. We were not disheartened though, but filled them again and again, well knowing that if we were saved from a death by asphyxia, tobacco would be the means. This was regular homeopathic treatment, but it was good for all of that.

But wood-smoke was not all we had to contend with. The heat from that circle of blazing logs made our tent a veritable oven. The sweat dropped from our bodies like rain, and it was a question with us if we would not have suffered less with the mosquitoes.

Absalom was uneasy. He would not stay inside the tent and he could not stay outside long at a time, and he was first inside and then out. He trotted about the circle sniffing the fire, at times evidently looking for a place to break through. My mind was in a condition similar to his, and if he, by a bold dash had shot through the flaming barrier, I believe I should have followed him, but I did not want to go first any more than the dog did.

Mr. Priour was as calm as death. He was rather warmer than cold, but that was all. I believe that man must have been a direct descendant of Shadrach, Meshach or Abednego, for with a tranquillity that was truly enviable he lay upon his blan-ket and slept as though housed at home.

There was more and purer air near the ground than elsewhere, but could I ever keep quiet long enough to get asleep? It did seem impossible, but at last it came. After having smoked and then buried my head in my blanket for the tenth or twelfth time, I entered a state somewhere between sleep and consciousness. I knew and thought nothing of tents or foiled mosquitoes, but of matters worse. I was in Tophet, and Priour and Absalom were with me.

Mr. Priour was seated on a blazing stump with feet stretched out and buried in a caldron of fuming liquid, his face bearing the expression of "this is rich; how lovely and warm it is here." Absalom was whining and trotting over the red-hot pavement as if in search of something he knew not what, while I was being tantalized by the negro whose dog I had helped steal. This fellow would open a door leading into clear cool air, and just as I attempted to pass out, he would slam it in my face, giving at the same instant a typical negro yell "Yah! Yah! He-yu! Steal my dog will yer, 'n' den lay it on de jecko. He! You! Who-yah!" I wondered why Mr. Priour did not come to my rescue and lay the fiend out, but he was too happy within himself to think of me.

Suddenly there was a shower of fire-brands falling all about us, a large one falling into Mr. Priour's lap, which he picked up and began to eat. Absalom dodged the brands which fell about him, but for some reason I could not do so, and finally when one of the coals dropped full in my face, I awoke with a yell that brought my partner also to his senses.

Smoke, smoke, smoke. Smoke from burning rags. Our tent was on fire. A large hole already in the roof, and soot and sparks falling all over our possessions, Priour's blanket and my own both sending up the odor of burning wool, while some of our choice specimens were contributing their share of perfume from the same causes. "Who set this tent afire?" shouted my companion, now fully awake. "We want water, and we want it quick, too!" Seizing the coffee pot he dashed its contents over the glowing rags, then with a bound he cleared the circle of fire, now much smaller than it had been, and quickly brought a supply of water from the Gulf. Ten minutes after my yell of pain, caused by a spark falling on my face, what remained of our tent was safe. The fire had been extinguished. I must have slept long, for the logs on the outside had burned down to less than half of their original bulk. The question now before us was who should sleep and who keep watch until daylight.

Mr. Priour was as kind-hearted a man as ever lived, and at his request I lay upon my scorched blanket, and was soon enjoying much pleasanter sleep than during the first half of the night, for it was cooler now and but little smoke came from the red hot logs. When I awoke again the sun was up, and Mr. Priour was rolled in his blanket by my side. We arose together, and the man explained that after sitting up a couple of hours and seeing no signs of more fire, he had turned in and enjoyed a good nap.

After breakfast our first work was to repair the tent. We had a grain sack nearly empty, and this was soon inserted where the flames had made an opening, with stitches large enough to be seen nearly as far as the tent itself.

Just why we thought it necessary to mend that opening I could not have told if put under oath. The grain sack was as porous as a sieve and would not have shed one drop of water, and whether we followed the dictates of reason or instinct I knew not, but at all events it was put over the hole.

WE GET OUT

The logs were yet aglow and the mosquitoes kept at a respectable distance from us. The scheme of making it too hot for these pests was a grand one, only we had overdone the matter a little and had made it almost too hot for ourselves.

The horses, turned loose the evening before, were nowhere in sight. I wondered how they had endured the attacks of the millions of insects, and thought they could not be blamed if now twenty miles from the Gulf. Mr. Priour was unconcerned about the animals and prophesied that old Whitie would be around for his grain in due time.

Tying Absalom to our wagon as a guard, we took a long walk down the Gulf shore. As soon as we had left the neighborhood of the fire the mosquitoes were upon us. But for all of their boring and probing, we secured many beautiful specimens of water birds. Least terns, royal terns, Caspian terns, marsh terns, sanderlings, kildeer plover, laughing gulls and turnstones were plentiful, and their plumage in the finest possible condition. Horned larks were also abundant about the tall grass, and being to my eyes one of the prettiest of small birds, I bagged a number of them.

We found our home guard still at his post of duty, but from appearances of the sand about him, he had been making strenuous attempts at liberty. How the dog could guard our things while he was bound to the wagon, fifty yards away from them, was another mystery connected with our modes of doing business, but he would not remain at camp unless he was so bound, so he was left to bark rather than to bite.

Fast Goers

Evening came and still the horses had not put in their appearance. I was a little uneasy about them, for of all places in which to be cast away and left without a team this was the worst.

"Now, don't you have a fit about them horses," said Mr. Priour. "I know where they are this minute, and can go and get them any time I want to."

"Where do you suppose they are?"

"They're at the mouth of the San Bernard Creek, that's where they are."

"How do you know that?"

"I know it dog-on'd well; they started down the Gulf last night. They can't get across though or they'd be in Corpus Christi before morning. They'll be here tomorrow sure; if they don't come I'll go after them; 'tain't more 'n' ten or twelve miles."

Mr. Priour was sure, and as he was a never-failing prophet, I was much comforted by his remarks. He did seem to have the faculty of guessing where his horses were at any time. His long experience in camping out, together with the known disposition of the horses to stray, had made him an expert in this way. A score of times I have known him to go straight to the lost animals when he had not seen them for twenty-four hours and when I had not the slightest idea in which direction they were.

This night we made the same arrangements with the mosquitoes as the last, but we had learned our lesson, and built a much smaller fire, at the same time increasing the size of the circle. Our modest blaze proved to be just as much protection as the tremendous conflagration of the first night, and we slept the sleep of the tired.

The following day we spent in hunting and in camp as before. An hour before sunset Mr. Priour called my attention to a moving object far down the Gulf.

"Do you know what that is?"

"A bear."

"No, sir. That ain't no bear; that's Whitie and Gruya, just as I told you they'd come home. They've been back to the San Bernard."

A half-hour later the two horses strode into camp, and such pictures of misery and despair as they presented I have never seen. The poor animals had been punished worse than their masters, and looked as though ready to drop from pain and exhaustion. They were covered with mud from head to tail, which mud, Mr. Priour said, they had accumulated while rolling to rid themselves of mosquitoes. Such expressions of penitence and grief I had never thought could be shown in an animal's face.

The condition of our team stirred us to a new thought: "Now, if you say so, I'll be dog-on'd if we don't leave here this very night. Them horses'll be dead by tomorrow morning from mosquitoes if we stay here."

I was ready to leave. We immediately fed the returned wanderers and struck our tent. It did seem a pity to abandon such a fine hunting ground, but I believed with my partner, that one more day at the place would have left us without horses.

Before it was quite dark we had crossed the grass plat and gone several miles beyond into the timber. There were few of the winged biters here and we made our bed without first making an oven to put it in.

CHAPTER XX
WE BUILD A FIRE

Early the next morning Mr. Priour made an important discovery. Gazing about in search of game he had seen a heron descend in the swamp miles away. "Now, when you see a heron go down among the trees do you know what it means?"

"No. What does it mean?"

"It means a good many things. It means first, that there's a lake or something out there; and it means that if there is a lake there, there's hundreds more herons roosting all over it. You'll find herons up there's thick's fleas, now, I'll be dog-on'd if we don't."

After breakfast a walk of two miles brought us to a lake or mud hole from fifty to a hundred yards in width, and, as far as we ever knew, from one end of the earth to the other in length. This body of mire was so completely filled up with small bushes and rank annual weeds that it was impossible to see across it in most places. It was boggy, but Mr. Priour crossed over on the shrubbery, and, one on each side, we proposed to search for game.

Beating the brush over in this place for two miles, we found herons in abundance. Snowy, little blue, yellow-crowned night, Louisiana and other herons apparently had the place for their headquarters. I killed nine or ten of these, and hearing Mr. Priour shoot quite often, supposed he was killing many more.

Alligators as Retrievers

This pond was also headquarters for hundreds of alligators, and as alligators like birds, and as the latter almost invariably fell in the mud when shot, I had to work actively to get my game after killing it. Sometimes I was too late and my prize would be seized and disposed of before I could climb over the reeking logs and snags to reach it.

Returning to camp I found my partner had brought fewer birds than I. He told me he had killed twenty or more, but as they had fallen into the mud among a thousand alligators he had thought best not to go in after them. He was surprised at the number I had taken, and thought they must have fallen on the land on my side. When I assured him that they had all dropped into the bog and that I had unhesitatingly gone among the alligators after them, he applied the term of "devilish fool" to me and said it was a wonder I had not lost a leg or two by my foolishness. "Fools step in where angels fear to tread."

After dinner we drove our caravan up by the side of the bog and camped again. Sallying out once more, we followed this narrow strip of miry mud several miles further than we had in the earlier part of the day. Herons were as thick as ever, but this time we troubled ourselves little for any but the snowy, and I was much more careful how I raced with alligators for the birds. Mr. Priour had "put a flea in my ear," and not wishing to lose a leg or two, I considered only that game as mine which fell quite near me. Toward night we discovered several nests of eggs of the herons in the tops of the bushes about fifty or sixty feet from shore, and Mr. Priour vowed he would have some of them if he hung for it. Having so many birds to skin, it was late when we turned in and also late when we turned out the next morning. Our first thoughts after rising were of the eggs we had found the night before, and after breakfast we went after them.

The bushes containing the nests were from an inch to an inch and a quarter in diameter, and were set not very close together. By a combined motion of leaping, sprawling and crawling over the top of the growth, we reached the nests without coming much in contact with the deep mud.

After filling our hats with eggs we looked wistfully toward the shore; it was still where we left it. In coming out to the nests, we had torn down and crushed all of the brush, shoved the logs and snags out of sight in the mire, and left nothing by which we could return. It looked as though we must ride back on an alligator or swim the bog. My temerity of the morning before had now been replaced by an equal amount of timidity; and as bad as it looked to crawl out over the brush and snags, it seemed ten times worse to wallow back through the element of reptiles. I asked good Mr. Priour to take me in on his back, but this he peremptorily refused to do. Presently my partner struck out for the shore by wading the boggy mud, and I resolved to follow him. All at once he disappeared and I wondered if he had made sound footing so quickly and reached the bank. Just at this time I saw what appeared to be a large alligator paddling around in the mud very near me, and I instinctively drew away from him. But he seemed to be heading for the shore rather than toward me, and watching closely I saw him crawl out on the land, pick up my partner's gun and start off toward camp. Then I saw my mistake. It was Priour after all, and shouting to him I cried: "Priour! Priour! How am I going to get out of this?"

"Get out of it any way you dog-on'd please!" he answered without halting or even turning his face toward me.

"Mr. Priour!" I shouted again. "Can't you drag some logs down for me to walk in on?"

At this request the man paused, faced about and said deliberately: "If you want any logs out there, come ashore and get them." Seeing Mr. Priour was thinking more of the camp than of me, I became desperate and jumped into the mud. My thoughts were wholly of the probability of my losing a leg or two, but after a short struggle with the black mixture in which I had jumped, I walked on the land unmutilated, and soon overtook my partner. When we returned to camp Absalom growled and gnashed his teeth at us. He would not recognize his master in that dripping garb, and at first it looked as though we might have a repetition of our Aransas River camp scene. But Mr. Priour was in no mood to be trifled with now, and marching up to the enraged animal he dealt him a blow with the butt of his gun that quieted him.

This experience had disgusted us with the locality and we decided to leave at once. We made quick time to Brazoria, and camped in the wood by the side of the river, where we proposed to spend several days in waiting for mail which was not yet due.

Our camp proved to be the most uninteresting place in which we had halted. Hardly a bird of value could we find. We secured a few hummingbirds, blue yellow-backed warblers and cuckoos, but these were hardly worth skinning. Our long-looked-for letters finally came, and one bright morning we drove to Columbia. We were nearly out of cotton, and had hoped to get a supply here; but at this time of the year cotton was not ripe and no one knew anything about it. We visited every store in the town, but were confronted at each by the same query: "Cotton? Cotton? What is cotton?" We showed the merchants samples of the little stock we had on hand and allowed them to examine it closely, but they all looked wise, shook their heads and said they could not remember having seen anything of the kind before.

After fiddling about Columbia until the middle of the afternoon, we left the place, and about a mile out met a party of men who had been traveling about the country for weeks in search of a place to settle with their families. They were social and we stopped and conversed with them for an hour or more. They were the first people we had attempted to hold a familiar conversation with for many days, and the halt by the wayside was an enjoyable one. Six or seven miles from Columbia we crossed a creek by a rustic bridge, and camped a short distance beyond. By the time we had eaten our supper it was quite dark, and we made a large and brilliant campfire for camping, which fire, from its position, was visible from the other side of the creek, only at the bridge.

Our Little Lantern

We had hardly spread ourselves before this cheerful blaze when we heard footsteps of a trotting horse across the stream. The animal seemed to be nearing the bridge by way of the road as we had done an hour before. All at once there was a sudden stump of the pounding feet, a snort and—"Hulloo dar! What de debil am dis? Git up dar! Git up dar! Doan be 'fraid dat fire! Git up dar ober de bridge!"

"Some cuss'd nigger," said my partner, "and his old plug's afraid of this fire."

"I suppose we can easily put it out," I said.

"Yes, we can, but we won't. I ain't going to put out my fire just so a nigger can go hen stealing. This is my fire."

While we were talking, the sounds of another and still a third horse could be heard coming up the road—thumpy, thumpy, thumpy; thump, thump, thump; thumpy thumpkerthumb—another snort—"Hulloo dar! What goin' on 'cross de kreak!"

There were three or four riders and horses now, and not one of the latter would budge an inch towards the snapping logs.

"Wha' dis here mean, Pete?"

"Good golly, I doan know, Sam."

"Dat some man wive a lantern," put in a third voice.

"My hoss ain' 'fraid lantern. Git up dar"—whack, whack, whack—"Git up, Bill."

Still they came—thumpy thump, thumpy thump—and we knew there must be something unusual on hand to call so many of these men out together.

"Hulloo, dar, ober de bridge!" shouted one of the negroes. "Put out dat lantern; we dun wan' go de weddin' up ole Bill Johnson's!"

Priour responded by piling a half-dozen more logs on the roaring fire, which sent a shower of sparks into the air that would have called out applause from a volcano. Then followed another discussion among the negroes.

"I tell yer dat ain' no lantern down dar; dat too big fo' lantern."

"Yes, dat be a lantern, too. I dun gone see two white men up Clumby dis yere day comin' out dis road."

"We no git de weddin' ter night dat lantern no blow out. Hol up dar dat lantern, Mister; we dun wan' git 'cross de kreak."

"Dem men sleep ober dar, Tom; you go ober 'n' see dey put out dat lantern. I hol' yer hoss."

While these words were being exchanged, Mr. Priour reached for his gun and pointing in the air, sent a double report roaring over the country. Instantly there was a wild uproar at the bridge, mingled with the pounding of feet from a dozen horses.

"Hol' on dar!"

"Hol' on; doan do dat agin!"

"Hol' on; my hoss dun gone git away!"

"O, dat too bad!"

"Dat lantern dun be too big for scare hoss."

"Dis yere debilish piece ob work I neber see!"

After order was somewhat restored, a new suggestion was made by one of the horsemen: They could blindfold their animals and lead them past the fire. This was an ingenious thought, and one that was soon put into execution; each individual divesting himself of his coat, throwing the latter over his horse's eyes and leading the creature quietly over the bridge.

Once the frightened beasts were beyond our blaze, several of the owners strode up to our camp to see "'bout dat lantern." We greeted them cordially. Mr. Priour stated that had he suspected anyone was annoyed by the fire, he would have scattered it at once. The two discharges of his gun he explained as being fired at a polecat which was bombarding us. Whether the negroes were satisfied with this explanation or not, I could not say, but believed they were skeptical. At any rate they rode away to the wedding.

CHAPTER XXI
JAM

Snakes

The following day we traveled slowly. At mid-day, our road entered a swamp and we halted for the remainder of the day. Near where we camped was a large and boggy bayou, and seated in the branches of a snag several yards from the bank was a negro with hook and line, patiently waiting for some fish to swallow his bait. He told us that the bayou extended up in the swamp ten miles further than any man had ever been, and that there were millions of snakes "up dar." He advised us by all means not to venture far from the road on account of them. But I was anxious to go, and, gun in hand, worked my way through the thick mass of vegetation for a half-mile, and crossed the bayou on a fallen tree. Birds were not aplenty, but I caught sight of a rabbit which I thought I would kill for our supper. Creeping up carefully, I was nearly within gunshot of the coveted game when I saw a large snake directly in front of me. I shot the snake and scared the rabbit, but still followed the latter with my eye. Creeping up a second time and getting within shooting distance, I was confronted by a second snake—a rattler. I killed this reptile and scared my rabbit again. Creeping up, a third time, I was met by at third snake which flattened his head and looked at me.

I had seen snakes enough before, but had never seen them so thick as here. I had thought little of these creatures when entering the wood, even when cautioned by the negro, but after nearly treading upon three within as many minutes, my eyes were on the lookout for them, and that swamp was veritably a snakes' paradise. While in the deepest and darkest part of my rambling, I believe I could have shot a dozen of the reptiles from any one stand. There were green snakes, black snakes and yellow snakes; snakes brown, gray, garnet, orange and pink; snakes on the ground, climbing the bushes and hanging from trees. I was less than a mile from the road, but was far enough. I did not care to discover the source of that bayou, and I carefully picked my way back to camp. Had I desired, I could have killed a hundred serpents on my way, but in my mind I said to each I saw: "If you'll only let me alone, I will you; and I'll never come in here again."

Mr. Priour had taken a tramp on the other side of the road, and although he had killed a few herons, the place did not prove to be such a fine one for birds after all. During the forenoon we had picked about a quart of dead-ripe blackberries, and as it was the first fruit we had seen for many days, we contemplated a delicious supper. I ate my berries just as they were gathered from the bushes, but Mr. Priour wanted his in a different way.

"Now, I tell you I can make the dog-on'dedest best jam that you ever put in your mouth. You don't know how to fix berries."

"You haven't anything to make jam with, have you?" I asked.

"Yes, I have," he answered. "I've got everything a man needs to make jam, and I'll soon show you something that'll make tears come in your eyes."

First, he put his berries into our stew-pot with some water and placed it over the fire. Next, he stirred in a handful each of salt and coffee—Mr. Priour was always fond of coffee. We had bought some tea and flour at Columbia, and a fair quantity of each of these was put in the pot, together with corn meal, pepper and some herbs from the swamp, which the man called bergamot.

After boiling for ten or fifteen minutes the jam was done, and its owner's face wore a pleased expression as he removed it from the fire. When it had sufficiently cooled, he swallowed a few mouthfuls of the mixture, but I noticed that he did not sail into it so ravenously as I had expected, and it was shortly laid aside altogether.

"What's the matter with the jam?" I asked.

"What's the matter with it? There ain't anything the matter with it, only it's rich and sweet. It's the best thing I was ever guilty of putting down my throat."

"I notice you don't put much of it down your throat."

"Well, if your head was aching like mine, I guess you wouldn't eat much of it; my head's pounding like a hammer."

"Let me taste of the jam."

"No, I won't let you taste of it; you gobbled your berries down in two mouthfuls and now you want mine; you can't have a sip of it."

"You are not very generous. That jam isn't doing you any good."

"No, but it will; my headache'll be gone in the morning and then I'll eat it."

The Much Enduring Absalom

After a long smoke we spread ourselves for the night as usual, but within thirty minutes and when I was about half asleep, I saw Mr. Priour slip carefully out of his blanket, steal up to his jam and deliberately upset the pot with his foot. Then, as I suddenly rose to a sitting position, the man grabbed Absalom by the neck, dragged him from under the wagon, beat him with a stick, and in strong language reprimanded him for overturning his pot of jam. Poor dog; he had not been within twenty feet of the compound and had not the slightest idea for what he was being punished nor why he should have been so ruthlessly snatched from his slumber.

"What's the matter now?" I asked.

"Matter enough! This cuss'd dog's been and rooted my jam over 'n' spread it on the ground here for a square acre or more."

"Can't you save any of it?"

"Can't I save any of it, you fool! Of course I can save it all! Of course I can scrape up a pot of coffee or a quart of water that's been poured over these leaves and sticks. Where did you get your education?"

"I thought Absalom was asleep."

"Well, I thought so, too, but he wasn't. He was just making believe so's to do this trick on me, and you're tickled to death that I've lost my jam after working so hard to make it."

The jam was now gone forever, and with seeming anger Mr. Priour sought his blankets again—this time for the remainder of the night.

In the morning I looked for the jam. I had made up my mind just what shape it would be in—one solid body like a heavy fruit cake. But I was too late; not a trace of it could I find. Mr. Priour had turned out at daylight, and the jam had probably been sent to the bottom of the boggy bayou.

CHAPTER XXII
A NEW USE FOR CHURCH BELLS

The most of this day our course lay through quite a thickly settled country, occupied almost wholly by negroes who tilled the soil of a hundred small farms. These farms bore fine looking crops of corn and cotton, and the people seemed prosperous and happy. The buildings were of logs roughly put together, but there was as much comfort and freedom per square foot as at any place we had seen. The roads were exceedingly tortuous, and many times we were compelled to drive four or five miles to make one or two in a direct line. It seemed to us as though we had to drive completely around every farm along our route. Every man that we interrogated in regard to our proper course gave us the same answer: "Keep de straight public road an' yer can' git loss." We did not see in our forenoon's drive a piece of road straight for more than twenty-five yards.

In the afternoon we drove through the settlement of Wharton, and at night halted at Spanish Camp—a long narrow slough which is the home of hundreds of alligators. The alligators in the slough bellowed all night long like a herd of wild bulls, and the mosquitoes sang symphony into our ears. Between the two, sleep was out of question until we were overcome by complete exhaustion toward morning. When we turned out, Whitie was on hand for his grain, but Gruya failed to show himself. This was rather strange, for the animals were not apt to stray from each other, and Mr. Priour surmised that Gruya had got into trouble somewhere down in the swamp.

Before eating breakfast we started out to hunt for him. Picking our way through briers and brambles, we followed the slough for nearly a mile, finding Mr. Gruya at last where he had spent most of the night. If there were spiders in Texas large enough to catch horses in their webs, I should have said that Gruya had thus been caught, for he was as completely encircled and bound by strong vines as if they had been woven with spider's skill about him. His two front feet were fastened together, and several coils of grapevine an inch or more in thickness were about his body and neck. He lay on his side in a bed of thorns and was as helpless as a babe. By a free use of our jack-knives the beast was liberated, and a half-hour later was eating a double allowance of grain.

At noon we camped near a settlement of white people. Here we intended to remain only an hour or two, to eat and rest our team; but when we were ready to hitch up, Absalom was missing. We spent an hour or more in hunting for him, but being unsuccessful, decided to wait his pleasure in returning to camp. Late in the evening the missing dog returned, and we tied him to a tree to make sure of his being with us in the morning. The tree held him fast and we were at liberty to move on the next day.

We Strike a Mill Race

Driving through the town of Eagle Lake we hoped to reach Columbus before making another halt, but about three miles from it, there were signs of an approaching storm, and we wished to get our things under our insufficient cover before it reached us. We were now near a small settlement, and by the side of the road was a grove of large and beautiful trees—just the place, we thought, for our camp. Pitching our tent under these trees, we got everything into it just as it commenced to rain, and we were much pleased with the appearance of our quarters.

It poured in violence, and we thought ourselves safe from all harm, excepting what water might leak through our roof. But soon the leaves on the ground began to wash away, and we then learned that instead of pitching our tent on level land as supposed, one end was on one side of a gulley, and the other on the opposite side. Great quantities of water were falling and in a short time there was a regular mill race running through our tent. Mr. Priour climbed a pile of boxes, and lying on his back across the top one, his outline shaped like a crescent, was soon asleep. In his position like a rainbow, with both extremities much lower than the middle, he would shed water much better than if straight.

While I was enjoying the rain, I heard a voice from the outside of the tent. Poking out my head I saw a negress clad in naked feet, bare legs, uncovered head and a very short dress.

"Has yer got any ladies or chilun in dar?" she asked.

"No," I answered.

"I didn't know but yer had er parcel oh young ones in dar. It am gwine ter run er stream in dar an' you'll git drownded out sho's de world."

"Yes. It runs in here now," I said.

"O, good golly! Dat ain' nuffin side what it be bam-by. Yer'd better dun git out dar; now I's a' tellin' ye."

This woman kindly invited us to come to her house and stop overnight. I thanked her for her good will, but we thought it best to stay with our property. It would not do to let our boxes remain under one dripping place too long at a time, and as we made it a rule to move each of them once in five minutes, we had to decline the invitation.

About 7 o'clock p.m. we sounded the river which had forced its way through our shelter, and though quite narrow, it was most too deep for our pleasure.

"Now, I tell you we've got to move this dog-on'd cabin ashore," said my partner. "It ain't a boat we've got if it is all tied up with ropes."

"We can't move now without getting everything soaked through," I answered.

"Well, they might just as well be wet by the rain as to be floated a mile down in the swamp, and then have to be fished out."

There was wisdom in Mr. Priour's remarks, and although the rain was pouring as hard as ever, we struck our tent and dragged it twenty-five or thirty yards to a higher and dryer place. During the time thus occupied, our luggage was freely exposed to the falling torrents, and before we were housed again with our treasures, everything was drenched as though fresh from the bottom of the ocean. This was not to be the first night we had slept with our clothing as wet as water could make it, and we spread our dripping blankets on the damp ground for our bed.

Columbus and Civilization

A clean and beautiful day followed the stormy night; such a day as would insure the drying of our clothes before they were slept in again; and spreading our blankets over the top of the loaded wagon, we journeyed on our way.

Columbus is situated on the Colorado River, and as we neared the stream it seemed as though we had been suddenly transported to a civilized country. The river is wider here than lower down where we had crossed before, and is spanned by a modern iron bridge that appeared altogether out of place in that region. The city, too, was different from any we had visited since leaving Corpus Christi; it was cleaner, better laid out, and the people we saw in and about the streets, as a rule, looked like reputable and moral citizens.

Driving through Columbus and ten or twelve miles beyond, we camped at noon near a small settlement known as Bordens. Leaving Bordens, we drove through Weimar and steered south toward Halletsville; but arriving at Oakland we learned that Halletsville was off our direct route, and that we could save time by going through Sweet Home instead. We were directed to a fork in the road a few miles beyond, where we would find a guideboard directing us to the last named place.

A Progressive People

Just out of Oakland we crossed Navidad Creek. Here there was a bridge which was undergoing extensive repairs. The overseer of this work had evidently heard something about pile drivers, and had improvised an apparatus to suit his own crude ideas. Having erected two post-oak logs as shears, he had borrowed the bell of the church at Oakland, which was doing the driving. By a simple whip purchase, some ten or fifteen men would hoist the bell by its clapper to the top of the shears and then let go the rope. The bell probably weighed seventy-five or a hundred pounds, and was astonishing the natives with its work in driving a pile into the soft mud. All Oakland had turned out to witness the operation of this labor-saving device. Every time the bell descended, the clapper struck the rim, and the sound thus produced was a stimulant to the vocal organs of the staring inhabitants; each descent of the borrowed weight, and the note thus produced, being authority for an untrammeled yell from every throat in the vicinity. There was no way of guiding the weight in its fall but by changing the obliquity of the shears, and as these were steadied by two lines held in a dozen pair of hands, the bell landed in the mud about as often as elsewhere.

At a modest distance from the workmen stood two rather aged negroes whose faces wore such expressions of tutored sedateness as can only be acquired by pastoral beings. One of these I took to be the clergyman of the Oakland church and the other probably a brother from another parish. They were commenting on the scenes before them, and during a pause in the labor and shouting I overheard some of their remarks: "It do beat all, what dis 'Merican 'Dependence do fo' de citizens ob de State. When Abraham an' Isaac digged der wells ob Beer-sheba, dey hab no 'ventions like dis."

"No, dey hab none ob dem ingines; an' when Josher an' de chillun ob Isrel cross ober de Jordan ter Canan, if dey hab been able ter buil' er bridge like dis, dey wan' no use for de riber run dry. It do seem ter me dat dey by 'n' by buil' er bridge ober de Guff ter der Jeruslum."

"No, sah. De 'Merican people can't be put down; dey is 'gressive. Dey buil' demselves bridges an' railroads, an' dere be glory for dem."

"Yes, sah. Dis am de lan' ob intellect an' good 'vancement ter de top. O, I be proud ob dis day fo' der colored man."

"DE 'MERICAN PEOPLE IS 'GRESSIVE"

CHAPTER XXIII
IN WHICH WE RETURN HOME

About a mile from the Navidad we came to a fork in the road; here was a guide-board which was to direct us to Sweet Home. The board was of native design and construction, and had I seen it in Boston, I should have thought of the Lone Star State. The manner of directing was unique, the letters being placed thus:

RIGHT HAND TO SWEET HOME
ELLIVTELLAH OT DNAH TFEL

Taking the right-hand trail we drove until nearly dark before coming to camp. In getting ready to sup this night we found that our kerosene can had been upset and its contents spilled over our crackers. We were hungry, and having on had no other food whatever, our meal was rather light but explosive.

The next day we drove through Sweet Home—so we were informed, but we could not locate the place. At night, our bed was made in a small clearing, surrounded by thick clumps of weesatche brush.

Our rest was uneventful until about 2 o'clock in the morning, at which time Mr. Priour gave a sudden shout and began throwing blankets and bedding in all directions. Hastily pulling off one of his boots, he turned therefrom an animal which had some resemblance to a crab; it had, though, too much tail for *Cancer* the crab, and proved to be *Scorpio* the scorpion.

My partner had received a thrust on his shin from this insect, and the latter quickly received a smart blow from a heavy boot that flattened him forever. The poisoned spot on the leg swelled quite rapidly and was painful, but an antidote in the shape of a tobacco poultice was at hand, and the patient spent the remainder of the night in applying and re-applying this soothing balm and in objurgating scorpions and "any man that was fool enough to live in such a cuss'd country as this."

"I wonder if there are any more scorpions around here," I said to the suffering man.

"Of course there is, you fool! Don't you know that scorpions travel in armies! There's a thousand of them within ten feet of you now."

"I didn't know they traveled in armies."

"Well, there's lots of things you don't know yet. Dog-on such a country as this; if there's any man living within a hundred miles of here, you can know he's a fool from the day he was born! You'll get stung forty times before morning."

I did not quite believe that there were a thousand scorpions within ten feet of me, but the circumstance of my partner's being wounded took from me all thoughts of sleep. This was one time when an animal had attacked Mr. Priour and had let me alone, but it was the only time during our whole trip. As I lay upon my blanket imagining a dozen scorpions and spiders creeping into my boots, one thought that came to me was: "Oh, for a lodge in some vast wilderness!" and I wondered if Brother Cowper had ever spent a hot June night in a Texan swamp.

We rolled about, smoked and talked until daylight, and after forcing down a few oily crackers, built a fire of what was left. They were completely saturated with kerosene, and were much better for fuel than for food.

This day we drove to Cuero, and hung about the post office from 2 until 4 o'clock p. m., waiting the arrival of the overland mail. We expected to receive mail forwarded from Brazoria and Gonzales, but left Cuero letterless, and driving until long after dark, camped about fifteen miles from Goliad.

About 3 o'clock the next morning we were called up by a heavy wind accompanied by a pouring rain, and quickly spreading our tent over the wagon, we crawled under. Fearing every minute that the high wind would carry our tent away to the top of some post-oak tree, we lay on the ground until the accumulating water compelled us to rest only on our feet. In this uncomfortable position we hoped to hold out until the rain should cease, but after a half-hour's trial Mr. Priour thought the imprisonment worse than getting wet. "Now, I'll be dog-on'd if I'm going to tie myself up in a knot and stay here a week just for a few drops of water. I never died yet by being wet." With these words he stepped out into the storm. I soon followed him, and within two minutes we were as wet as the rain itself.

A House in the River

By daylight the sky was clear again, and after making a breakfast of coffee, we were once more on the way to Goliad. The rain had left the roads disgustingly muddy and our horses could not trot a step, so we made slow time. Shortly after our start we were met by an enormous number of white wood ants which were on the wing. Flying through the air they resembled a thick snow storm, and many of them losing their wings on the way, the road in places was strewn with thousands and thousands of the disarticulated members in a single drift. I believe I could have scraped up a quart or two of them as well as not.

In the afternoon we drove through Goliad, crossed the San Antonio River, and camped for the night on the prairie about ten miles beyond. There being no water in our vicinity, we went supperless to bed. In the morning we started off with empty stomachs, driving until noon, when we halted on the prairie near a mudhole.

In the afternoon we drove through Refugio, and at night camped six miles from the town, near Willow Creek. This stream had just been supplied with a brand new bridge, and bridges are dispensed sparingly in this part of the State. About 10 o'clock in the evening and just as we were about to close our eyes for the night, a "nigger team" drove up to the creek. The driver had evidently never seen a bridge before.

"Whoa dar; what de world am dis yere! Some cuss'd fool been done gone an' buil' er house right in de middle ob de road; nuffin done yit but de flo'. Good mind t' dribe right ober de thing. Hulloo dar! Who own dis house!"

"I own that house," shouted Mr. Priour, springing to his feet and rushing out to the bridge, "and I'm going to put a roof on it tomorrow. What do you want here anyway?"

"I done wanna git crost dis yere kreak. Wha' fo' yer buil' a house on dis yere kreak?"

"I want it so I can lay abed and fish through a hole in the floor."

"He-you! I neber heerd tell ob dat style afore. But I wan' a git crost, I done wan' a go de Mission."

"If you want to get across you'll have to drive through the water down below here."

"Good golly! Dis de wors' piece ob business I done seen yit; but I doan care, my horse done go fru dis water afore."

After the negro had driven through the stream a few yards below the new "house," Mr. Priour came back to his bed and went to sleep.

The Last Push of the Trip

The next noon we camped on the bank of the Aransas River, near what is known as the Aransas Reef. This river was very boggy, but teams had crossed it, and Mr. Priour said that wherever a white man had been, a man from Corpus Christi could go, and he was going to cross here. The stream was about four hundred yards in width, the water about two feet deep, and beneath was from two to two and a half feet of soft mud.

Unhitching and mounting Whitie, Mr. Priour started across on an exploring tour. About one-third way to the other side, his horse bogged and he was obliged to dismount; he continued on his way, however, and spreading his trousers and boots to dry on the other bank, came back wearing simply his hat and shirt. Harnessing up again, our team was driven into the muddy mire. We attempted to assist the horses by heaving, one at each side, but as we could easily turn the wheels around in the mud by one finger, no good could be done in this way. In fact, we had about all we could do ourselves to keep from sinking out of sight. I felt tolerably safe as long as I had one hand on some part of the wagon, and it was hard for me to let go of it when occasion required. One who has never been bogged cannot know the feeling that comes over a person when sinking in the mud with both feet as useless as though in irons, and no alternative but to roll over on the side or fall and thus paddle out. A dozen times this afternoon

I heartily wished my partner was not so willing to go anywhere that any white man had gone,

After plunging and rearing about for a half-hour the horses struck work; they had hauled the wagon nearly half-way across, and were exhausted by their exertion. I did not blame them. It was a wonder to me that they had not balked long before—they had not balked this time, but were too tired to go further. They were now loosened and driven ashore by Mr. Priour, while I climbed the wagon and seated myself for a smoke. A short rest recuperated our horses and they were again driven into the slough and attached to the load. Another half-hour's struggle and we were safely across the foul river, but as completely covered with mud as was possible to be, without smothering. Further up the stream we found a little clear water, and washed some of the soil from our faces, but our clothing we decided must dry on our persons before the dirt could be disposed of. Near where we had crossed there were evidences that someone had bogged to their extinction; a large funnel-shaped hole being visible, which Mr. Priour said was probably the bier of some bogger. He informed me that it was not uncommon for people to break through the dry coating of mud near the firm land, and never get out again.

Two miles from this river we came to a stretch of rough and open country, between which and the Aransas Bay were hundreds of acres of marshy land. Laughing gulls were abundant here, and we took as many specimens as we could use. Driving several miles beyond this marsh, we camped in the identical spot we had occupied on the tenth of April.

The whole of the next day was spent in skinning our birds and growing hungry. We were out of provisions entirely and had swallowed little but coffee for twenty-four hours. At 6 o'clock p. m. "the last dog-on'd bird" had been skinned; and harnessing our team, we started for Corpus Christi, thirty-five miles away. The night was moonlit, and after eight hours of driving we reached the town and our headquarters.

During the first week after our arrival at Corpus Christi we spent the greater part of the time in eating. Mrs. Priour was a good cook, and we kept her busy. Between our meals, however, we were quietly making preparations for another hunting tour, and by the time we had quieted the longings and yearnings which had been growing in our stomachs for several weeks, we were ready to leave Corpus Christi again.

ONE MORE RIVER TO CROSS

CHAPTER XXIV
A CRUISE ON THE MUD FLATS

From a man who lived by the waters of Nueces Bay we rented a sailboat, at four bits a day. This boat—the *Reuthinger*— was a homemade affair about 30 feet in length, carrying a mainsail and jib. Toward the stern, a place was partitioned off, which the owner said was a cabin. One most excellent quality about this cabin was the ventilation; it was perfect, especially on the top, and there could not, under any circumstances, be danger of our breathing impure air while on this ship.

One bright morning, old Whitie and Gruya took our supplies of ammunition and provisions two miles through the brush, and down to the edge of the bay where the *Reuthinger* was sitting in the soft mud—the *Reuthinger* would sail through mud as well as water—and using a small boat as a sort of sled, we slid ourselves and our luggage to the vessel. To get our goods aboard was the work of but a few minutes, and soon the anchor was on deck and our sails set to the breeze.

The bay contains only a few small islands but an abundance of reefs of shell, from one inch to two feet below the surface. The water is not deep at any place but is supported by soft mud which is of unfathomable depth. Into this bay empties the Nueces River, and at the junction of the two is a mud flat, miles in extent. The river is deep and narrow, but at its mouth spreads out, as it were, to cover this great surface with an inch or two of water. The amount of water over the flat depends in a great measure upon the direction of the wind; a breeze from the east sends the water from the bay over the shoals, while a strong current of air from the west will have an opposite effect and leave the crest of the flat above the water's edge.

From various sources I learned that years ago the bay had extended several miles further back than now, and that the boggy soil on the sides of the river was at that time just such a flat as the one I have described. If this is true there is no reason why the whole bay may not in time be replaced by land. Such a radical change as this is to be hoped for, for if there are seventy-five square miles on this earth that disgrace it, those seventy-five square miles may be found here, Nueces Bay being one big slimy slough, only fit for the habitation of alligators and mudsnakes.

A strong east wind favoring us, we made good time to the head of the bay, and this same wind made it possible for us to enter the river's mouth. Our boat drew about six inches of water, while there was not more than two inches over the flat; but with such a breeze—all the *Reuthinger* could stand—we plowed our way through the mile of mud, a furrow high and dry being turned up on each side.

Slow time was made through the obstruction, our boat often coming to an apparent standstill. Once over in deep water, we could see by the winding furrows the exact course we had taken.

The Crew Goes Overboard

Running up the stream a short distance, we came to anchor in ten or fifteen feet of water. The land for miles about us was dotted here and there with small patches of coarse grass and rushes, but these, with the hundreds of drift-logs lying about, did not cover one-half of the surface exposed to us. This naked soil was covered by a dry crust about a half-inch in thickness, which gave to it an appearance of solidity, but it didn't take us long to learn that to step off a sod or snag was nearly equivalent to stepping into unoccupied space. There was much more of vegetable life near where we had anchored than elsewhere. Shortly after we had furled our sails, I thoughtlessly jumped to what I supposed was the shore, but immediately found myself up to my armpits in mire, and had not good Mr. Priour come to my rescue, I should have sunk to solid bottom four miles below.

We needed some kind of a stopping place on the river's bank, and collecting a large quantity of driftwood, built a circular platform twenty feet across, with an extension down to our boat. There was an abundance of logs and snags along the river's edge as far as we could see, and over these we could travel in perfect safety. They had drifted from the Nueces Bottoms miles above, and but for their presence our shooting would have all been done from on board our boat.

We tramped over the sods and rushes a little but did not often venture far from the line of driftwood. Foster's terns, least terns, black-headed gulls, willets, snipe, etc., were plenty, but we refrained from killing any that were over the mud. When we came to this place we had but about two or three gallons of fresh water, and the close of our second day left us without a drop. The water of the river was not strong of salt, but was just brackish enough to fail completely to quench thirst. Boiling coffee in the liquid made it taste even salter than in its natural state, and on the evening of the third day we were as thirsty as if we had drunk nothing for twenty-four hours. The next day we were dryer than ever, and I spent more time in reckoning the amount of pleasure in a cubic inch of water, than I did in hunting. We had as many birds as we needed, but were waiting for a fair wind down the bay, for we had grave doubts about being able to get over the flats with any but a stiff breeze behind us. But at midday we determined to try to get out of the scrape even if the wind was ahead; we had suffered from thirst just enough to be ready to try anything that might lead to the moistening of our throats.

Getting the *Reuthinger* underway, we beat down the river to the flat. The furrows we had made in coming in had by this time disappeared, but it would not have been necessary for us to follow them had they remained visible, and with

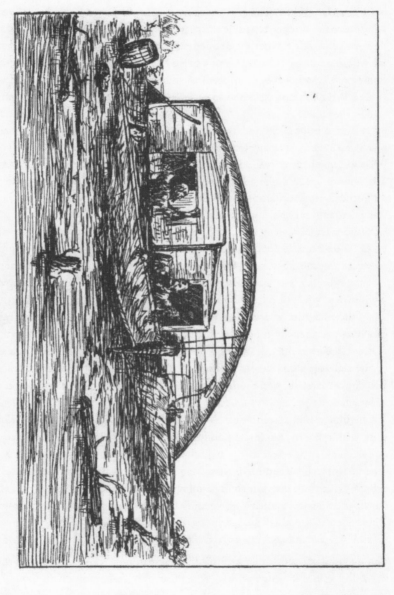

WHERE THERE'S LIFE THERE'S HOPE

close-hauled sheets we courageously ran our bow plump into the mud. This
stopped our headway, but it didn't ease the wind nor light up our sheets, and
before we could guess what was taking place, our boat swung broadside to the
wind, careened to her beam's ends and dropped Priour and myself into the mud
to our necks. But for our caught-on-the-fly holds of the capsized vessel's cabin,
we would never have seen Corpus Christi again, and we soon climbed to that side
of the craft which was now uppermost. Our sails were daubed with mud and our
anchor had slid overboard and sunk to the length of its line, but our guns were
safe in the cabin.

"Now I'll be dog-on'd if this ain't a sweet mess," said my partner, "any man
that'll make a fool of himself by coming into such a place as this deserves just
what we've got, and I'm ready to lay here and die."

"I don't want to die in any such hole as this," I answered.

"Well, then, go on ahead and pull this box through the mud; I'll stay here and
steer her."

"Can't we right her up?"

"Of course we can. You go out there and stand in the mud and lift up on the
mast; I'll pull on the riggin' here; that's the only way we can do it."

"I should think we might do it by putting everything on the topside and weight-
ing it down."

"So should I. You go down and bring up the anchor; you can find it by following
that line, and then we'll hang it over the side."

After debating the question five or ten minutes we went to work on the job
of righting our ship. She had settled six or eight inches in the mud, but as she
was decked over for eighteen inches from the sides, there was no danger of her
sinking.

Our first move was to try to scoop out a place in the mud on the windward
side, with a board, hoping she might right herself by dropping into the cavity,
but as quick as one boardful was scooped away, another took its place, and this
scheme had to be abandoned. Next, one at the bow and the other at the stern, we
dropped over into the mud, and paddling with our feet and legs, slowly wormed
the boat half way around a circle; this bringing her with her deck toward the
wind.

In the Doldrums

The mainsail was then unbent from the boom, and the latter swung far out over
the vessel's side. Raising on the mast a little, and slackening the toppinglift, gave
us a good purchase, and going out to the end of this spar, we played see-saw with
the *Reuthinger*. The boom was rather a slender one, but the toppinglift took the
most of the strain, and after swaying a half-dozen times upon this lever, we saw
our boat gradually assuming the upright posture. Soon she was level again, and

bending our sail on to the boom once more, we went off before the wind and sailed up the river to our late anchoring ground.

We had been away from here about three hours and returned with some little information and a great deal of mud. Our deck and sails were in a most filthy condition, but Priour advised that we wash neither of them until finally over the flat. We both wished someone could tell us when that time would be, for we were satisfied that the *Reuthinger* would never beat through that bar. If the owner of the boat could have seen her when we came to anchor the second time, he would never have recognized her as his own.

We had no thoughts of hunting now, and after rinsing our clothes by a plunge into the river we stretched ourselves on the deck to dry and to thirst. Our only hope was that the wind might soon change to the west, and we repented the day we left home with such a small supply of water. Every drink that I took from the river seemed saltier than the preceding ones, and one more day, I thought, must make me too disgusted with its brackishness to touch another drop. We had eaten nothing since morning and wanted nothing in the line of food, and in the evening we spread ourselves on the *Reuthinger's* cabin floor. I could not sleep a wink, and I knew by my partner's frequent change of position that his rest was of little good to him.

After rolling about until nine or ten o'clock, I crawled out of my blanket and went on deck. Mr. Priour soon followed me. The air was as calm as death, and seating ourselves on the cabin we discussed our situation. I asked my partner if the water was not fresh further up the stream. He said that with an east wind it was salt for a long distance, and although we might easily sail up with a fair wind, we could never get down with a head one, the stream being too narrow and too full of snags for our boat to beat in. About three or four miles up the country, he said, there was grass-covered land which had at one time contained numerous small ponds of fresh water. He didn't know whether they held water at this time or not, and the way there was dangerously boggy.

Mr. Priour evidently was not suffering so much from the want of water as I, but after a little persuasion he consented to accompany me on foot up to the place he had described. I was willing to walk, swim, paddle through a bog or do anything else in order to get a drink of water. Taking our lantern and coffee pot, we set out on this tramp. Following the river's edge and treading almost wholly on the snags and driftwood which had been washed on shore, we beat our way over the bottomless mire. We encountered several obstructions in the form of bayous, which connected with the larger stream; but into these we tumbled large snags, making bridges by which we could safely cross. The river was as crooked as the letter S, but we could not leave its curves, and it must have been long past midnight when we reached the grassy land which afforded solid footing.

Mr. Priour seemed to know every square foot of the country here; he had been over it many times, and when once clear of the mire he quickly led the way to the depressions in which he had seen water. The first one visited was dry; so was the second, the third and the fourth—the tenth and all intervening ones, and it looked as though our exertions had all been in vain. But after visiting twelve or fifteen of these small hollows, we found one which contained a few inches of liquid. This was full of wrigglers of a hundred species, but what cared we for them? They didn't affect the taste in the least, and prostrating ourselves, we put our lips to the shallow pool and drank, drank, drank; drank until we could hold no more.

We remained about here a half-hour or less, drinking every few minutes, and when fully satisfied, filled the coffee-pot and headed down the river again. Our return was simply a repetition of our earlier walk, only there were no bridges to build this time, and we reached our boat just as a streak of light had begun to show itself in the east. We were tired now, and rolling in our blankets, were soon asleep.

We Start Again

Several hours after the sun had risen, I was awakened by my partner, who in gleeful words was telling me the wind had hauled around to the west. He could have said nothing more agreeable to my ears, and after a hasty lunch of crackers and fresh-water coffee, we made ready for sea.

The wind was in our favor at last; it was blowing a good breeze too, and in our minds we saw the noble *Reuthinger* plowing through the flat, leaving behind a stream of mud like smoke from a locomotive. How we would yell in imitation of the shriek of a steam whistle, and startle the alligators and garfish from their beds as we cut through their unresisting homes! "Onward!" was our battle cry, and we were pawing the earth in anxiety for the fray. We did not stop to wash any breakfast dishes this morning, but hoisted our anchor, raised our sails and got underway. Priour took the helm, and with a look of firm determination, boldly steered the craft down the narrow stream. But as we rounded a bend, the man's expression of resolution gave way to a look of anxiety.

"Well now, I'll be dad-gon'd and back again; just look there."

"Look where? I don't see anything."

"Don't see anything?! Can't you see that mud flat two feet out of water! How're we going to get out of here when the wind's blown all the water out of the bay?"

"Can't we plow through as we did before?"

"As we did when, yesterday? Don't you know, when the wind's to the west all the water goes out of this hole! You're one fool and I'm another!"

"What shall we do now?"

"What shall we do? What can we do? I'm going to ram this old scow into that mud her whole length, and then we can't do anything but stay there!"

"We'll be as bad off then as we were before."

"Yes, and worse off; but I'm going somewhere, and it ain't back to any Nueces River either. When we fetch up, you'll land twenty feet ahead of the boat, and you can go on to Corpus afoot."

When plowing through this bar on our way to the river's mouth, we had not realized that a west wind which would be fair for our return, would drain the water from the bay to such an extent as this, nor that we were plowing our way into a veritable trap. Of course the water from the river could not enter the bay without passing over the flat, but as the latter was miles in extent, there might be forty small canals through it without our knowing their whereabouts.

I Have Faith in Priour

Mr. Priour did just as he declared he would do, and ran the boat straight into the bank, which was full six inches above the water's surface, and as we came to a sudden stop, our sails were dropped on deck. I didn't land twenty feet ahead of the boat, but would have gone overboard had I not prepared for the jerk. Mr. Priour was under as much headway as myself and came near taking the tiller into the cabin with him.

"There," said the man as he regained his balance, "now we're here and we'll stay here till the wind changes. We ain't going over that mile of cow pasture with the wind to the west, and a north wind won't be a bit better."

"We can't get over with a head wind; we've already tried that," I said.

"We'll go over with a head wind or we'll stay here and rot. Head wind, fair wind, or no wind, we can't sail this box on dry land; that's all there is about that."

Having great confidence in my partner's ability to cope with the most unpromising circumstances, I felt that sooner or later all would be well. Mr. Priour was not easily frightened, and had learned to believe he could find some way out of any kind of a scrape.

We had water enough for the day at least and plenty of food; and as there was nothing in particular to do, we passed the time in various unprofitable ways.

There was a 20-foot pole about the ship, but we couldn't push with it any more than if in twenty feet of water; however, we thought of a plan by which we could make it of use to us. Taking one of our boxes to pieces, we fastened a board securely on one end of the stick, with some strings and nails found on board the boat. This gave us two square feet of surface to push with, but we were not to use this appliance until the wind had gone down and let the water over the bar.

At sunset the sky became cloudy and the air much calmer, and we watched the edge of the flat, to note any rise of water. It did rise a little, and with it our hopes, for we were going over the flat if it took all night to do so, and every rise of a half-inch was so much in our favor.

At nine o'clock the wind had entirely died out and the top of the flat was nearly covered with water. A fine drizzling rain was falling and the night was of inky darkness. All things considered, it would have been much pleasanter to turn in and sleep than anything else, but we knew our duty and were not to shrink from it.

The *Reuthinger* did not carry a compass, but Mr. Priour was confident he could instinctively find the way over the flat. This feeling I shared with him, for he was well acquainted with every spat of land and water in Nueces County, and had acquired the faculty of guessing right, ninety-nine times out of a hundred, whenever uncertain just what step to take. Bringing forth the pole that had been rigged for the occasion, we dropped the reinforced end into the mud, and applying our united strength, the *Reuthinger* slid through the slime the length of our stick. The latter was then slowly drawn in over the stern, and the movement repeated. This labor we kept up for a half-hour, and as the boat seemed to slide forward easier at each succeeding motion, we believed the rain was assisting us.

The Chips Tell the Story

We were now willing to pause a while and rest, for although the work was not hard, it was tiresome. During this recess, I lighted our lantern and brought it on deck, and my partner, in order to learn of the amount of water that had come to our rescue, held the light over the stern of our boat. No sooner had the struggling rays fell over the surface of slime, than a stream of loud words issued from the man's mouth.

"Oh! Dog-on! Dad-gon! Dig-gon! We're a hundred fools from Mudtown! You're a fool and I'm your brother!"

"What's the matter?" I asked.

"What's the matter?! What's the matter! What's the matter! Look over this boat! Look there! *Look there!* LOOK THERE!"

I looked over the side of the boat in the direction pointed out to me, but the only things I saw were some chips of wood.

"I don't see anything to be scared at," I said.

"Don't see anything to be scared at?! Neither do I, but don't you see them chips?"

"Yes, and what of them?"

"What of them! Do you know what chips they are? They're the ones we threw overboard this morning when we's fixing that pole!"

"How came they down here?" I asked.

"How came they here, you idiot! They're right where they've been all the time! We've been sliding this old tub back and forth for an hour and ain't gone a foot, and I can lick any man on the boat."

"I thought we were shoving her ahead."

"I know you did, and we did shove her ahead and then pulled her back again with that paddle. Here's a pond we've made for her to float in; no wonder she went easier every time," and tearing our new paddle apart, the man threw the board far out into the darkness.

Thirty minutes of work in the rain had been wasted, but after we—especially one of us—had calmed down somewhat, another plan was proposed and tried.

We had a small skiff with us which we could get through the mud by vigorously working the oars, and with this we took the *Reuthinger's* anchor as far ahead as possible and dropped it overboard; then going back to the large boat, we hauled ourselves up to it. The line on the anchor was about fifty feet in length, and the addition of our main sheet gave us as much more. There was no sliding backward this way, and each trip with the anchor in the small boat was equivalent to our advancing the length of the lines. But this labor was arduous in the extreme; the small boat was heavily loaded each time, and it required our utmost strength on the oars to move it, and as it took fully fifteen minutes for the completion of each cycle, independent of breathing spells, we realized that our task was to be a long one.

Steamboating

Leaving our lantern on board the large boat, we occasionally rowed the skiff some little distance astern between the turned up furrows, and with the assistance of the light, were able to form some idea of whether or not our course had been direct from the start. We knew how our ship was heading when the sun went down, and our escape from the trap now depended on keeping the furrows straight. It would have been discouraging to have worked all night getting the boat into water, and in the morning have found ourselves in the mouth of the river again, and we spent no small amount of time sighting over our wake. Without the lantern this would have been impossible, but with it, all was well. Two hours of such labor as this, with the rain above and the mire below, took some of the heroic ambition out of us, and we fumbled our brains for new suggestions.

"Now I'll be dog-on'd if this ain't the worst scrape you ever dragged me into," said my partner as we seated ourselves on the cabin to rest, "and I don't want to kill myself getting out of it, either."

"How far do you suppose we've gone?" I asked.

"We ain't quarter way over yet, and I'm going to try another trick; I believe we can paddle her like a steamboat."

I was ready to try anything for a change, and sticking our pole in the mud and hanging the lantern to it, we dropped over the boat's stern and began to paddle with our feet. At first I was a little skeptical about our being able to make any headway in this manner, but as our distance from the light gradually increased, I knew we were doing well. This was much easier than by the anchor process and our advance more rapid.

About midnight, lunch and tobacco were served and a half hour's rest taken, when we dropped over the stern to our work again.

After two or three hours more of churning in the clammy slime, we were delighted to see symptoms of water. This was as a stimulant to our tired legs and arms, and an hour after the first signs had been noted, the *Reuthinger* was afloat. Taking the skiff ahead, we now towed the large boat on, until she was a foot above the bottom and then, mud and all, we dropped upon our blankets and fell asleep within three minutes.

It was after sunrise when we opened our eyes and came on deck again, and the sight that first met our eyes would have paralyzed a soapmaker. The poor *Reuthinger* was plastered with mud from stem to gudgeon; not a spot of the original boat could be seen, and we needed shovels and hoes to begin work with. Our supply of fresh water had given out the night before, and without breakfast we sailed the craft into deeper water and began our work of cleaning ship. It would never do for the vessel to go back to her owner in any such condition as this or we could never rent her again. The sails were unbent and put to soak while we were scrubbing the deck, cabin and hold, and after exerting ourselves for two hours or more, most of the mud had disappeared.

The wind was light, but fair for our course, and raising the wet sails we headed down the bay. By the middle of the forenoon we were back at the place where we first boarded the boat.

CHAPTER XXV
HARD-EARNED DUCKS

A week after returning from our cruise in the *Reuthinger* we had recovered enough strength and courage to be stimulated to another journey. This was to be an overland trip; I had had enough of the water for a while and so had my partner.

Above the junction of the Nueces River with the bay the river is bordered on each side by a strip of timber several miles in width—the Nueces Bottoms. The bottoms are dark and gloomy; every particle of ground not occupied by the large and magnificent trees is covered with shrubs and tall palmetto leaves; while the direct sunlight is almost completely shut out by the long and flowing Spanish moss which covers every tree, weaving their twigs and leaves together in a tangled and matted web. But for the many roots which form a network beneath the surface, all this land would be too boggy to uphold any living creature, and at the channel's sloping sides, where but few roots are present, it is dangerous to venture away from snags and logs.

Under a section of this grand leafy canopy Mr. Priour and myself drew our wagon one bright and cheerful day, prepared to spend a week and do the swamp. Shortly after our arrival we crossed the stream and, followed by Absalom, plunged into the chaotic expanse of vegetation. My partner was used to this scenery and thought little of its grandeur, but at first I was much more interested in this spectacle, so fit for admiration, than in looking for game. Hawks and owls were common, but owing to the compactness of the trees they were not easily obtained. Ducks were not just in our line, but there being few other birds in the bottoms, we decided to try for them.

Mr. Priour knew more of duck hunting than did the fowl themselves, and after tearing through the brush for about half the distance to be traveled we dropped on our hands and knees to creep. The man's judgment was good, and although we had not seen the ducks since our start, we cautiously drew ourselves up to the edge of the waterway directly over the game. The bank was indeed steep, it was more than vertical, having been undermined by the water's action when the stream was swollen.

One thought that came in my mind was, that after shooting the birds we would be unable to get them; for no man could walk over that bottomless mire, or even mount the cliff after being at its base. But oral communication was not in order, and as my partner motioned for me to shoot, I did so in unison with him. There were about a dozen of the fowl feeding in the pool, and when the smoke had cleared away we saw that five of them remained.

Spider Tactics

"Now how are you going to get them out of that mud?" were the words that left my lips.

"Now don't you fret about getting them out," came the reply. "I've hunted in this country too much not to know enough to pick up my game."

"But that mud won't hold up a pound, will it?"

"Not not an ounce, and I don't propose to get into it either. I'm going down on them vines on that tree there, like a spider on his web."

Just on the edge of the bank there stood a large sycamore tree well-furnished with tangled vines, which were woven among the branches and extended from the ground to the leafy dome above. These vines hung from branches which projected ten or twelve feet over the cliff, but they were not long enough to reach to the mud below. To remedy this shortness, the rope-like stalks were pulled in toward the bank and our united weight surged upon them a dozen times. This so loosened and stretched the fastenings aloft that the briery snarl descended far enough to reach the level twenty feet below. I was glad it was my partner and not I that was going down on such a ladder. It would have been a rare bird indeed to tempt me to undertake such a journey; but if there had been but a shoestring to descend by, it would have been all the same to the reckless Texan.

Weaving his body well into this vegetable web, the man cast himself from the bank and began his spider-like descent. He was, though, less dexterous than the average spider, and several times, through the slipping of some strand, it seemed as if he must soon shoot head-foremost into the bog; for while not intentionally imitating a spider in descending upside down, he was not always able to make choice of position, his feet being at the top nearly half of the time. My heart was in my throat during this performance, until the man dropped safely onto a lone snag near our birds, when I breathed much easier.

Once on firm footing, Mr. Priour drew each fowl to him with a long stick, and threw them, one by one, on the bank at my feet. Then entering the wickerwork again, he began the ascent. He had descended in safety, and it seemed as if he should as safely return but the fates had decided otherwise. After he had climbed six or eight feet, one of the vines gave a little, then another gave a little, another and another, until the whole concern appeared to be losing its grip on the tree.

The man had the best of courage and redoubled his efforts. Up, up, up he struggled, sometimes gaining on the descending vines, and sometimes losing. For several minutes he thus bravely battled in mid-air, and though crawling over many feet of slipping briers, he still kept only about ten feet from the snag below. It appeared to me as if he could climb on for a month, and that the thorny ladder had no end; but finally it was completely unravelled, and with a spank-like sound the man dropped into the mud below, and was buried by the coils and mats of leaves, twigs and brush that came falling on his head. Quickly scraping this woody shower beneath him, he raised himself erect, evidently no worse for the fall.

"Now I'll be dog-on'd if that riggin' ain't completely unbusted!" he exclaimed. "But it held on longer'n I thought 'twould. I didn't think 'twould hold till I got halfway down here."

"How are you going to get out now?" I asked, for there were no other vines near, and I saw no possible way for deliverance.

"Well, I'll load my pipe and have a good smoke and you can go back to camp and bring the harness lines. They'll hold me, any way."

I was perfectly willing to go after the lines, but it was such a new country to me, and the scenery presented so much sameness, that I had doubts about being able to find my way alone. But that was the only thing that could be done to succor my friend, and after receiving most specific instructions from him as to the course, I turned and left his presence.

On a snag in the middle of a boggy stream, twenty feet below the surface of the earth, was a dreadful position to be left in, and well knowing the responsibility, I quickened my steps toward camp. It was now about two or three o'clock in the afternoon, but as no direct sunlight came through the trees there were no shadows cast, and I had no way of keeping my course but by dead reckoning. Mr. Priour knew every square foot of the wilderness, but I was the same as on the ocean without rudder or compass.

After tearing through the braky bottoms for an hour and seeing no signs of another stream, I became suspicious that all was not right. I had but about a mile and a half to go in all, and should have covered that distance in less time than I had been on the way. Still, there was nothing to do but to travel on; even if lost, I couldn't return to my partner any better than to camp, and it would be useless to return to him anyway.

Another hour passed and yet no stream. If I could only have climbed a tree and lifted my head into daylight, I could probably have learned something of my whereabouts; but they were all so large that such schemes were quashed as soon as thought. I was now getting quite discouraged, and was no better off than if on a snag in the river; but as "Somehow or other the pathway grows brighter just when we mourn there are none to befriend," a feeling of relief soon crept over me, for I had suddenly found the stream. This I quickly crossed, and from the angle at which its general course had met with mine, I knew on which hand our camp must be—miles away. I was far up the river, and another half-hour's battle with the brush found me at camp.

It was two and a half hours since I had left the other fork, and getting the harness lines I at once crossed the stream, and again entered the swamp on my mission of mercy. It would have been nothing strange had I again lost my way, but this time I had rather better luck. I did not go straight to my destination, yet gained time on the last tramp, and an hour after leaving camp had reached the second stream. To find the bluff where I had left the helpless man was not so easy, but after coursing up and down the bank for a while I recognized my situation and was soon nearing the spot where I had been four hours before.

Approaching the steep bank, I cast my eyes over the muddy flat below, while a shudder passed over my body. The snag and vines were there, but no sign of life. My partner had gone.

Could it be that he had rolled off the log and sunk forever? Could it be that he was now being digested in the stomach of some huge reptile? Had I not known him well, I should have thought that something such was the probability; but the man was not one of the dying kind, and after composing myself I could but think that he was safe in some part of the bottoms. There were no signs to show that he had left the snag, but this soft mud would hold imprints hardly better than water, and I thought little of their absence.

It was now getting late in the day; at best, I could not easily reach camp before dark, and bidding *adieu* to the vicinity, I started to cross the swamp for the fourth time that day. I was now a little better acquainted with the country, and an hour later reached river number one. Crossing this, I strode into camp, where, lazily reclining by a fire, was the man I had worked so hard to rescue from the boggy pit.

"Now I'll be dog-on'd if I wouldn't like to know what you're swampin' back and forth with them lines for; you're as full of business as a bee-hive."

"How long have you been here?" I asked.

"I've been here long enough to make a pot of coffee and drink it."

"And how did you get out?" I continued.

"Now don't ask too many questions all at once. When I get into a scrape I generally get out again somehow, and if I'd waited for you to fish me out with them lines I'd been there for a year."

I asked no more questions, but Priour's condition told me more than words could do, for he was mud and slime from top to toe. If he had been a wick, and the mud tallow, I could have lighted him and he would have burned all night.

The next morning, after breakfasting on our well-earned ducks, we took to the woods again. This time we followed the river, entering the swamp but a little distance; for there were more birds about the water, and less of brush and palms to wade through.

About a half-mile below our camp we found three lone goats bogged in the nearly dry river bed, where they had evidently been for several days. The land all about this part of the country is divided up into pastures containing many square miles each, which are occupied by thousands of sheep, goats, horses and neat cattle. These animals obtain water from the river, and many are annually lost by bogging while after drink. The goats we were anxious to rescue, but as they were unapproachable we were at loss to know just how to do it. Mr. Priour finally solved the problem, and sent me back for the ever-useful harness lines. I did not lose my way in getting them, and was soon back with the articles. Had it been otherwise, and some delay caused in returning, I should have expected the man to play alligator and boldly enter the mire.

Of course my partner was expert at throwing lines; otherwise he couldn't have retained the individuality of a Texan, and with little trouble a noose was soon thrown over each animal's head, and they were snaked out of the slump. Their necks bore the strain much better than one would dare suppose, for although it required our utmost combined strength to dislodge them, not a bone snapped nor a head unfastened.

"Now I tell you I ain't a jerkin' out goats for nothing," said my companion, "and I'm going to have my pay for this work."

"Send a bill to the owner?" I asked.

"No, sir; no bill about it. I'm going to take my pay in milk for my coffee, and this here animal's going to furnish it."

How to Milk a Goat

Milk I very seldom saw in Texas, for it is usually beneath the dignity of a native to abstract it. To run a coon through the brush, to be stripped naked by prickly-pears while hunting hogs or to be soused in the mud in securing ducks is all very well; but quietly to sit and milk a cow, is employment too effeminate for a hunter to engage in. I believed the only reason why this man wanted milk was because he knew he would have to fight in order to get it.

The goat had never been milked by human beings, nor was it used to being led; but by a mixture of dragging, driving and leading, the animal was finally brought into camp. The first drop of fluid extracted brought a rear and a kick which sent the coffee pot from the milker's hands and the "dog-ons" from his mouth, and he found it necessary to tie one of the animal's legs to a tree. But this was only a beginning. Soon another leg was thus dealt with, then another and another, till the beast lay upon its back as fast as if in a straightjacket.

After a deal of trouble, about a gill of milk was secured, and the prisoner was released, when she darted off through the trees happy to be free again. This adventure spoiled the forenoon for us, and during the afternoon we were at camp making ready for a longer journey to be begun on the following day.

Wild turkeys were the birds wanted on the morrow, and to find them we must cross the wilderness to its far side and there prepare to remain all night. Mr. Priour rolled up the wagon sheet and strapped it to his shoulder as his part of the baggage, while I carried a lunch and our coffee pot, the latter crowded with tobacco, pipes, coffee and matches. Our course through the timber was anything but straight, and it was full two hours before the second river was before us. As was expected, here we met with trouble, for although the stream was narrow, it was not supplied with snags upon which we could cross. My partner predicted that further down its course we would find the waterway much wider and more snaggy.

Beating our way through the deep-tangled wildwood for two or three miles toward the bay, we reached that part of the swamp where the two rivers united at an acute angle. Here there was an entire change of scene. Instead of a narrow channel bordered by steep banks, there was a spread of mire acres in extent, wherein thousands and thousands of snags and water-soaked logs were piled in confusion.

Snakes Galore

More than this, hundreds of snakes were to be seen about and upon the drift-wood, where they had come to bask in the sunshine and to feed in the shallow pools. Nearly every snag supported at least one reptile, and I thought that before attempting to cross we would have to clear our intended path with powder and shot. These serpents were not all of one species, but moccasins were the pre-dominating kind.

While here, I had the opportunity of seeing one of the slimy beings capture and swallow his food. The shallow pools swarmed with small fish an inch or more in length, and, leaving the extremity of his tail upon the uncovered mud, the snake swung his head out into the water, and describing the arc of a circle, brought his neck and fore parts upon the bank a foot or more from his tail. This maneuver inclosed many of the fish between the slimy body and the shore, when the reptile turned his head into the circular inclosure and fed at his leisure.

Arming ourselves with short and heavy clubs, we left the solid earth for the boggy river bottom. Of course Mr. Priour was in the lead, and springing and leaping from one snag to another, he not only cleared the latter of snakes, but showed the way for me to follow. He assumed, however, much more risk than I was willing to, and several times lighted upon logs which immediately sank beneath his weight. But he was no more afraid of mud than of air, and profited nothing by such happenings.

I had hoped to cross without soiling my clothes, and possibly might have done so but for a trick played upon me. I was many feet behind my companion, and just as I was in doubt as to whether or not it would be well to leap upon a log that had failed to support him, the man put on a terrified expression and shouted, "Look out, look out for that snake!" I had expected to be bitten by one of the reptiles before getting half-way across, and that shout, coupled with the warning, completely upset my fine adjustment. No sooner had the words left his mouth than I sprang upon the questionable log. In an instant I was up to my neck in the slough, and had not the author of the mishap quickly come to my rescue, I should have been there yet.

"Where's the snake?" I asked as soon as I had been dragged upon firm footing.

"What snake?"

"The snake you told me to look out for."

"Now, I wasn't talking to you at all, I was speaking to Absalom. Ha, ha, ha!"

We reached the solid earth across the stream and were in a forest where the trees were fewer in number and the undergrowth of weeds and palm leaves much less abundant. Under the drooping branches of a noble willow tree we made our halt and built a campfire. We were both hungry and tired, and when the lunch had been disposed of, spread ourselves to smoke and to sleep.

We Dine on Turkey

It was after sunset when we came to our senses again, and leaving under the tree the few articles which had been brought, we set out for the turkey haunts. Mr. Priour was familiar with the habits of these birds, and some little distance from our recent stopping place stationed me under the branches of a small clump of trees.

Leaving me at this place, my companion disappeared in the direction of another grove a mile distant. The two groves, he had informed me, were the ones most likely to be occupied by the desired game, and that the latter had probably already arrived at his trees. He expected to get a shot at them first, and that they would then come to my grove and give me the same privilege.

In due time I heard two shots in immediate succession, and although already completely screened under some low brush, I instinctively crouched into a still smaller space. Soon I heard the sound of beating wings, and a moment later the branches over my head supported a dozen or more of the noble fowl. I was much more anxious to secure a male than a female; but the night was too dark to be able to distinguish one from the other. I aimed at one of the largest, and as the uninjured birds were sailing away, winged another with my second barrel. This fluttered off through the underbrush, and with gun in one hand and my dead turkey in the other, I darted in pursuit. The fleeing bird was not much injured, and led me a long chase, but was finally captured.

Retracing my steps, I met Mr. Priour at my late hiding place. He bore three birds on his shoulders, one male and two females, while I had one of each sex. It might seem highly improbable that the game in question should have come to the very tree under which I was stationed, when there were others all about the place; but Mr. Priour had hunted turkeys in this forest and stood under those very trees many a time, and knew from much experience just where they would go after the first assault upon them.

We soon found our way to camp, and building anew the dying fire, made coffee and ate another lunch. Our turkeys were all plump and in good plumage, and I was much pleased with the result of our evening's work. Setting out the next day, in due time we reached our original camp. Here we skinned, cooked and ate of our wild turkeys.

I Heed the Lesson

The next morning we bade the Nueces Bottoms an *adieu*, and by midday had reached an open and naked prairie. But little rain had fallen here for some time, and the few cattle to be seen feeding about were very thin.

Making a halt in the edge of the bush we fed our horses and ourselves, and then took a stroll in search of game. About a half-mile from our halting place and some little time since I had last seen my partner, I was pleased to discover two white-tailed hawks sitting close together on a bush much more than a gunshot away. These birds were quite desirable, and I determined to try for them. Creeping slowly, and carefully working my way through the tangled vines and briers for at least five or ten minutes, I approached as near as the dense thicket would allow. I was still rather a long gunshot away from the coveted prize, but couldn't entertain thoughts of giving them up after so much labor. It would be but a charge or two of ammunition wasted anyway, and possibly I might wing one of the birds.

Taking careful aim and bringing the gun to bear on them, I let go both barrels. This act brought commotion enough—ten times more than I had dreamt of; for simultaneously with the discharge the two hawks shot off uninjured, two fiery eyes under my partner's hat shot up above the brush about halfway to where the birds had been, and a score of angry words shot straight into my ears.

"Oh, I'll be dog-on'd, dog-on'd! What're you shooting at birds for a mile away! Didn't you know I was sneaking up to them hawks? I could killed them both if you'd only kept quiet and minded your own business."

"I didn't see you," I replied.

"You didn't see me! Well, you didn't see them birds when you fired, if you looked where your gun pointed!"

"Yes, I did."

"Now I'll be dog-on'd if you did! You can't see through my hat, for there ain't no winder in it!" and holding his headgear aloft, he exhibited a dozen holes which had been made by shot from my gun.

"Now I tell you," he continued. "'tain't no fun for a fellow to crawl a mile and a half through the hedge like a snake, and then have a double-barreled cannon fired into his head just as he gets ready to shoot."

This admonition had a temporary effect on me, and I withdrew from my companion's near vicinity. I allowed him plenty of room to crawl a mile and a half through the hedge like a snake, in any direction he pleased, and as a result he brought into camp two large and plump sandhill cranes. These birds are edible, their flesh being fit to fatten a king, and we had as good assurance of a juicy supper as could have been desired. Never again did I undertake to shoot game through my partner's hat.

A Sad Ending

Suicide of Dr. Arthur C. Peirce at Riverside.

SHOT HIMSELF IN THE LEFT BREAST AT HIS HOME.

Act of Self-Descruction Followed Nervous Breakdown.

HE HAD BEEN UNABLE TO PRACTICE FOR OVER TWO YEARS

Financial Reverses Followed in the Train of His Illness, the Whole Combining to Make Him Exceedingly Despondent. – His Wife, Who Had Been Away During the Afternoon, Found the Body on the Floor on Her Return.

Dr. Arthur C. Peirce, formerly a leading and successful physician in Riverside and vicinity, committed suicide by shooting himself in the left breast, at his home, corner of Bullock's Point and Oak avenues, early last evening. Dr. Peirce, who was about 45 years of age, and who had for two years and a half been unable to practice because of breaking down of his health, was alone in the house at the time he committed the act of self-destruction…Literally driven to the wall financially, unstrung by his long illness and perhaps resorting to some powerful antidote to deaden his realization of his desperate condition, he resorted to the bullet. It was a sad ending of a career which had promised much only a few years ago.